Instant Vortex Plus Dual Air Fryer Cookbook UK

Effortless and Healthy Air Frying Quick, Crispy & Delicious Meal Recipes-Master Your Instant Vortex Plus with Easy-to-Follow Instructions

EVA S. CANNON

TABLE OF CONTENT

Day	Breakfast	Lunch	Dinner
1	Blueberry Muffins with Streusel Topping	Crispy Chicken Tacos with Avocado Crema	Lemon Herb Salmon Fillets
2	Apple Cinnamon Oatmeal Cups	Beef and Cheese Quesadillas	Cajun Blackened Tilapia Fillets
3	Breakfast Burritos with Crispy Bacon	Crispy Mozzarella Sticks with Marinara Sauce	Herb-Roasted Whole Chicken
4	Air Fryer French Toast Sticks	BBQ Chicken Quesadillas with Pepper Jack Cheese	Juicy Air Fryer Burgers with Cheese
5	Banana Walnut Bread	Coconut Shrimp with Mango Salsa	Garlic Butter Steak Bites
6	Breakfast Egg Rolls with Ham and Cheese	Spinach and Artichoke Dip with Tortilla Chips	Crispy Chicken Parmesan with Marinara Sauce
7	Chocolate Chip Pancakes	Crispy Fish and Chips with Tartar Sauce	Moroccan Spiced Lamb Koftas
8	Mini Quiche Cups with Spinach and Cheese	Avocado Egg Rolls with Cilantro Lime Dip	BBQ Baby Back Ribs with Homemade Sauce
9	Cinnamon Sugar Donuts	Classic Chicken Wings with Buffalo Sauce	Mediterranean Stuffed Trout with Feta and Olives
10	Sausage and Egg Breakfast Sandwiches	Crispy Pork Chops with Apple Compote	Sweet Potato Wedges with Cajun Seasoning
11	Breakfast Pizza with Eggs and Bacon	Crispy Buffalo Cauliflower Bites	Honey Garlic Glazed Salmon Fillets
12	Veggie Breakfast Hash with Eggs	Garlic Parmesan Breadsticks	Italian Sausage and Peppers
13	Breakfast Sausage Patties	Sweet Potato Fries with Sriracha Aioli	BBQ Chicken Drumsticks
14	Blueberry Crumble Bars	Coconut Crusted Shrimp with Mango Salsa	Rosemary Garlic Roast Beef
15	Air Fryer French Toast Sticks	Crispy Asian Spring Rolls with Sweet Chili Sauce	Lemon Garlic Roast Chicken Drumsticks
16	Apple Cinnamon Oatmeal Cups	Homemade Potato Chips with Dipping Sauce	Garlic Butter Mushrooms with Thyme
17	Crispy Breakfast Potatoes	Cajun Fried Chicken Drumsticks	Mediterranean Roasted Eggplant Slices
18	Breakfast Pizza with Eggs and Bacon	Cheesy Garlic Breadsticks	Moroccan Spiced Lamb Koftas
19	Chocolate Chip Pancakes	Crispy Mozzarella-Stuffed Meatballs	Spicy Korean BBQ Beef Short Ribs
20	Banana Walnut Bread	Coconut Shrimp with Mango Salsa	Juicy Air Fryer Burgers with Cheese

Day	Breakfast	Lunch	Dinner
21	Mini Quiche Cups with Spinach and Cheese	Crispy Onion Rings with Spicy Dipping Sauce	Italian Herb Chicken Parmesan
22	Sausage and Egg Breakfast Sandwiches	Sweet Potato Wedges with Cajun Seasoning	BBQ Baby Back Ribs with Homemade Sauce
23	Veggie Breakfast Hash with Eggs	Spinach and Artichoke Dip with Tortilla Chips	Garlic Parmesan Chicken Wings
24	Blueberry Muffins with Streusel Topping	Crispy Chicken Tacos with Avocado Crema	Herb-Roasted Whole Chicken
25	Breakfast Burritos with Crispy Bacon	Avocado Egg Rolls with Cilantro Lime Dip	Spicy Tuna Poke Bowls with Avocado
26	Apple Cinnamon Oatmeal Cups	Crispy Fish and Chips with Tartar Sauce	Lemon Herb Salmon Fillets
27	Cinnamon Sugar Donuts	Beef and Cheese Quesadillas	Crispy Chicken Sandwiches with Coleslaw
28	Chocolate Chip Pancakes	Garlic Butter Steak Bites	Sesame Ginger Glazed Mahi Mahi
29	Breakfast Egg Rolls with Ham and Cheese	Sweet Potato Fries with Sriracha Aioli	Lemon Pepper Shrimp Skewers
30	Air Fryer French Toast Sticks	Classic Chicken Wings with Buffalo Sauce	Moroccan Spiced Lamb Koftas

INTRODUCTION

Welcome to the world of air frying with the Instant Vortex Plus Dual Air Fryer! This innovative kitchen appliance has revolutionized the way we cook, allowing us to enjoy crispy, delicious fried foods without the guilt and mess of traditional deep frying. With its advanced dual air frying technology, the Instant Vortex Plus delivers evenly cooked, crispy results every time, making it a must-have for health-conscious individuals and busy families alike.

Air frying has taken the culinary world by storm, and for good reason. By using rapid air circulation and precise temperature control, the Instant Vortex Plus Dual Air Fryer can mimic the crispy texture and flavor of deep-fried foods with little to no oil required. This not only reduces the calorie and fat content of your favorite fried dishes but also eliminates the potential dangers and mess associated with deep frying at home.

One of the standout features of the Instant Vortex Plus is its dual basket design, which allows you to cook two different foods simultaneously without any flavor transfer. Imagine having crispy fries and juicy chicken tenders ready at the same time, without the hassle of separate cooking sessions.

With the Instant Vortex Plus, you'll also experience faster cooking times, easier cleanup, and a more compact and energy-efficient appliance compared to traditional ovens or deep fryers.

In this cookbook, we've curated a collection of mouth-watering recipes that showcase the versatility of the Instant Vortex Plus Dual Air Fryer. From classic comfort foods like crispy chicken wings and loaded potato skins to gourmet dishes like coconut-crusted shrimp and herb-roasted whole chicken, you'll find a wide range of options to satisfy every craving.

So, let's embark on this culinary journey together, where every bite is a celebration of flavor, crispiness, and the joy of eating well. Get ready to discover a world of possibilities with the Instant Vortex Plus Dual Air Fryer, where crispy perfection meets effortless convenience.

TIPS FOR USING THE AIR FRYER EFFECTIVELY

To ensure you get the most out of your Instant Vortex Plus Dual Air Fryer, here are some valuable tips that will elevate your air frying experience to new heights:

1. Preheat, preheat, preheat: Always preheat your air fryer before adding any food. This crucial step ensures that your food cooks evenly and develops that perfect crispy texture we all crave. Just like preheating an oven is essential for baking, preheating your air fryer is the key to achieving optimal results every time.

2. Don't overcrowd: Resist the temptation to cram too much food into the air fryer basket. For best results, arrange your food in a single layer, leaving some space between pieces. Overcrowding not only leads to uneven cooking but also prevents the hot air from circulating properly, which is the secret to achieving that coveted crispiness all around.

3. Shake or flip: Certain foods, like french fries, chicken wings, or vegetables, benefit from being shaken or flipped halfway through the cooking time. This simple step ensures that every piece is exposed to the hot air, preventing sticking and ensuring even browning on all sides.

4. Use oil sparingly: While air frying requires little to no oil, a light misting or brushing of oil can enhance crispiness and flavor. Much oil can defeat the purpose of healthy air frying. Consider using an oil mister or a silicone brush to evenly distribute a thin layer of oil over your food.

5. Experiment with seasonings: Air frying is a fantastic way to bring out the natural flavors of your ingredients, but don't be afraid to experiment with different spices, herbs, and marinades. From zesty lemon pepper to smoky paprika, the possibilities are endless.

6. Master the timing: Every air fryer is slightly different, and cooking times can vary depending on the amount and type of food you're cooking. Keep a close eye on your food, especially during the initial few uses, to gauge the perfect cooking time. Remember, you can always add a few extra minutes, but you can't undo overcooking.

7. Let it rest: Just like with traditional cooking methods, allowing your air-fried food to rest for a few minutes after cooking can make a big difference. This resting period allows the juices to redistribute, ensuring that your dishes are perfectly cooked.

8. Clean regularly: Proper maintenance is key to ensuring your air fryer performs at its best. After each use, make sure to clean the basket, crisper tray, and any other removable components to prevent buildup and ensure optimal air flow for your next cooking session.

By following these tips, you'll unlock the full potential of your Instant Vortex Plus Dual Air Fryer, creating crispy, delicious, and healthier versions of your favorite fried foods with ease. Embrace the art of air frying, and get ready to impress your family and friends with every perfectly cooked dish!

SAFETY PRECAUTIONS AND GUIDELINES

While the Instant Vortex Plus Dual Air Fryer is designed with safety as a top priority, it's essential to follow these precautions and guidelines to ensure a worry-free cooking experience every time you use this innovative appliance.

1. Read the manual: Before you even think about plugging in your air fryer, take the time to thoroughly read the instruction manual. This comprehensive guide not only provides valuable insights into the appliance's features but also outlines crucial safety information and operating instructions. Familiarizing yourself with the manual will help you avoid potential hazards and ensure that you're using your air fryer correctly from the start.

2. Keep it clean: Maintaining a clean air fryer is more than just a matter of hygiene; it's a safety measure. Always ensure that the air fryer and its components are free from residual food particles or grease before use. Leftover debris can create a fire hazard, potentially leading to dangerous situations.

3. Don't overcrowd: While it might be tempting to maximize each cooking session, overfilling the air fryer basket can have severe consequences. When the basket is overcrowded, food can come into direct contact with the heating element, increasing the risk of fire or personal injury. Follow the manufacturer's guidelines for recommended food quantities and resist the urge to overload the basket.

4. Use caution when handling hot surfaces: The Instant Vortex Plus Dual Air Fryer and its accessories can become extremely hot during operation. Always use oven mitts or tongs when handling the hot basket, crisper tray, or any other components. Avoid touching the exterior of the air fryer during and immediately after cooking, as the surfaces can reach high temperatures.

5. Unplug when not in use: While it might seem like a simple step, unplugging your air fryer when not in use is crucial for safety. Even when the appliance is turned off, leaving it plugged in can pose a potential fire risk. Develop the habit of unplugging your air fryer after each use and allowing it to cool completely before cleaning or storing.

6. Keep a safe distance: During operation, the Instant Vortex Plus Dual Air Fryer releases hot air through its vents. To prevent accidental burns, keep your face and hands at a safe distance from these vents. Additionally, ensure that the appliance is placed on a stable, heat-resistant surface, away from combustible materials like curtains or tablecloths.

7. Monitor during use: While the air fryer is designed for convenience, it's essential to monitor it during operation. Never leave the appliance unattended, as unexpected situations can arise, such as smoke or overheating. Staying close by will allow you to respond promptly and take necessary actions if required.

By following these safety precautions and guidelines, you can enjoy the many benefits of the Instant Vortex Plus Dual Air Fryer with peace of mind.

CRISPY BREAKFAST POTATOES

Prep: 10 mins | Cook: 20 mins | Serves: 4

Ingredients:

- 750g potatoes, diced into 1-inch cubes

- 2 tbsp olive oil

- 1 tsp garlic powder

- 1 tsp paprika

- Salt and pepper to taste

Instructions:

1. Preheat your Instant Vortex Plus Dual Air Fryer to 400°F using the Air Fry function.

2. In a large bowl, toss the diced potatoes with olive oil, garlic powder, paprika, salt, and pepper until evenly coated.

3. Place the seasoned potatoes in the air fryer basket in a single layer.

4. Air fry the potatoes for 15-20 minutes, shaking the basket halfway through, until they are crispy and golden brown.

5. Once done, remove the potatoes from the air fryer and serve hot.

Nutritional Info: Calories: 180 | Fat: 7g | Carbs: 26g | Protein: 3g

Tip: For extra crispiness, soak the diced potatoes in cold water for 30 minutes before seasoning and air frying.

Prep: 10 mins | Cook: 10 mins | Serves: 4

Ingredients:

- 8 slices of thick-cut bread, preferably stale

- 3 eggs

- 120ml milk

- 1 tsp vanilla extract

- 1 tsp ground cinnamon

- Maple syrup for serving

Instructions:

1. Preheat your Instant Vortex Plus Dual Air Fryer to 375°F using the Bake function.

2. Cut each slice of bread into strips to form French toast sticks.

3. In a shallow bowl, whisk together the eggs, milk, vanilla extract, and cinnamon.

4. Dip each bread stick into the egg mixture, ensuring they are well-coated.

5. Place the coated bread sticks in the air fryer basket in a single layer.

6. Air fry the French toast sticks for 8-10 minutes, flipping halfway through, until they are golden brown and crispy.

7. Serve hot with maple syrup for dipping.

Nutritional Info: Calories: 220 | Fat: 7g | Carbs: 30g | Protein: 9g

Tip: For a variation, sprinkle some powdered sugar or drizzle chocolate sauce over the French toast sticks before serving.

Prep: 15 mins | Cook: 15 mins | Serves: 4

Ingredients:

- 8 small flour tortillas
- 8 slices of bacon
- 120ml milk and 6 large eggs
- 1 bell pepper, diced
- 1 onion, diced
- 100g shredded cheddar cheese
- Salt and pepper to taste
- Chopped fresh parsley for garnish

Instructions:

1. Preheat your Instant Vortex Plus Dual Air Fryer to 375°F using the Air Fry function.

2. Lay the bacon slices on the air fryer tray and air fry for 8-10 minutes until crispy. Remove and drain on paper towels.

3. In a bowl, whisk together the eggs, milk, salt, and pepper.

4. Heat a skillet over medium heat and scramble the eggs until just set. Remove from heat.

5. Assemble the burritos by placing a spoonful of scrambled eggs, diced bell pepper, onion, crispy bacon, and shredded cheese onto each tortilla.

6. Fold the sides of the tortilla over the filling and roll up tightly.

7. Place the assembled burritos in the air fryer basket seam side down.

8. Air fry the burritos for 5-7 minutes until they are golden brown and crispy.

9. Serve hot, garnished with chopped parsley.

Nutritional Info: Calories: 380 | Fat: 22g | Carbs: 25g | Protein: 20g

Tip: Customize the burritos with your favorite toppings such as avocado, salsa, or sour cream.

Prep: 5 mins | Cook: 10 mins | Serves: 4

Ingredients:

- 400g pork sausage meat
- 1 tsp dried sage
- 1/2 tsp garlic powder
- 1/2 tsp onion powder
- Salt and pepper to taste

Instructions:

1. Preheat your Instant Vortex Plus Dual Air Fryer to 375°F using the Air Fry function.

2. In a bowl, combine the pork sausage meat with dried sage, garlic powder, onion powder, salt, and pepper. Mix until well combined.

3. Divide the sausage mixture into 8 equal portions and shape them into patties.

4. Place the sausage patties in the air fryer basket in a single layer.

5. Air fry the sausage patties for 8-10 minutes, flipping halfway through, until they are cooked through and golden brown.

6. Once done, remove the sausage patties from the air fryer and drain on paper towels.

7. Serve hot as a delicious breakfast side.

Nutritional Info: Calories: 260 | Fat: 20g | Carbs: 1g | Protein: 18g

Tip: Make a batch of sausage patties ahead of time and freeze them for quick and easy breakfasts.

Prep: 15 mins | Cook: 15 mins | Serves: 6

Ingredients:

- 6 large eggs

- 120ml milk

- 100g baby spinach, chopped

- 50g grated cheddar cheese

- 1/2 tsp garlic powder

- Salt and pepper to taste

- Chopped fresh chives for garnish

Instructions:

1.   Preheat your Instant Vortex Plus Dual Air Fryer to 350°F using the Bake function.

2.   In a bowl, whisk together the eggs, milk, garlic powder, salt, and pepper until well combined.

3.   Stir in the chopped baby spinach and grated cheddar cheese.

4.   Grease a muffin tin and pour the egg mixture evenly into each muffin cup.

5.   Place the muffin tin in the air fryer basket and air fry for 12-15 minutes until the quiche cups are set and golden brown on top.

6.   Once done, remove the quiche cups from the air fryer and let them cool slightly.

7.   Garnish with chopped fresh chives before serving.

Nutritional Info: Calories: 110 | Fat: 7g | Carbs: 2g | Protein: 8g

Tip: You can customize the quiche cups by adding other ingredients such as diced ham, bell peppers, or mushrooms.

Prep: 15 mins | Cook: 20 mins | Serves: 12

Ingredients:

- 200g plain flour and 120ml milk

- 100g caster sugar and 1 large egg

- 2 tsp baking powder and 1/2 tsp salt

- 60ml vegetable oil and 150g fresh blueberries

For the Streusel Topping:

- 50g plain flour and 50g granulated sugar

- 50g cold unsalted butter, diced

Instructions:

1. Preheat your Air Fryer to 350°F using the Bake function.

2. In a large bowl, mix together the plain flour, caster sugar, baking powder, and salt.

3. In a separate bowl, whisk together the milk, vegetable oil, and egg.

4. Pour the wet ingredients into the dry ingredients and mix.

5. Gently fold in the fresh blueberries.

6. Divide the batter evenly among 12 muffin cases in a muffin tin.

7. In a small bowl, combine the plain flour, granulated sugar, and cold unsalted butter for the streusel topping. Use your fingers to rub the mixture together until it resembles coarse crumbs.

8. Sprinkle the streusel topping over the muffin batter in each case.

9. Place the muffin tin in the air fryer basket and air fry for 18-20 minutes until the muffins are golden brown and a toothpick inserted into the center comes out clean.

10. Once done, remove the muffins and let them cool.

Nutritional Info: Calories: 200 | Fat: 8g | Carbs: 30g | Protein: 3g

Tip: These muffins are best enjoyed warm with a cup of coffee or tea.

Prep: 15 mins | Cook: 45 mins | Serves: 8

Ingredients:

- 250g plain flour and Pinch of salt

- 1 tsp baking powder and 2 large eggs

- 1/2 tsp baking soda and 1 tsp vanilla extract

- 1/2 tsp ground cinnamon and 100g light brown sugar

- 2 ripe bananas, mashed and 50g chopped walnuts

- 100g unsalted butter, melted

Instructions:

1. Preheat your Instant Vortex Plus Dual Air Fryer to 320°F using the Bake function.

2. Grease and line a loaf tin with parchment paper.

3. In a large bowl, sift together the plain flour, baking powder, baking soda, ground cinnamon, and salt.

4. In another bowl, mix together the mashed bananas, melted unsalted butter, light brown sugar, eggs, and vanilla extract until well combined.

5. Pour the wet ingredients into the dry ingredients and stir until just combined.

6. Fold in the chopped walnuts.

7. Pour the batter into the prepared loaf tin and spread it out evenly.

8. Place the loaf tin in the air fryer basket and air fry for 40-45 minutes until a toothpick inserted into the center comes out clean.

9. Once done, remove the banana walnut bread from the air fryer and let it cool in the tin for 10 minutes before transferring to a wire rack to cool completely.

Nutritional Info: Calories: 280 | Fat: 12g | Carbs: 38g | Protein: 5g

Tip: Serve slices of banana walnut bread toasted and spread with butter for a delicious breakfast or snack.

Prep: 10 mins | Cook: 20 mins | Serves: 4

Ingredients:

- 2 large potatoes, diced

- 1 onion, diced and 1 tsp paprika

- 1 red bell pepper, diced

- 1 green bell pepper, diced

- 2 tbsp olive oil

- 1 tsp garlic powder

- Salt and pepper to taste

- 4 large eggs

- Chopped fresh parsley for garnish

Instructions:

1. Preheat your Instant Vortex Plus Dual Air Fryer to 375°F using the Air Fry function.

2. In a large bowl, toss together the diced potatoes, onion, bell peppers, olive oil, garlic powder, paprika, salt, and pepper until well coated.

3. Spread the seasoned vegetables evenly in the air fryer basket.

4. Air fry the vegetable mixture for 15-20 minutes, shaking the basket halfway through, until the potatoes are crispy and the vegetables are tender.

5. Once the vegetables are cooked, create 4 wells in the mixture and crack an egg into each well.

6. Air fry for an additional 5-7 minutes until the egg whites are set but the yolks are still runny.

7. Garnish with chopped fresh parsley before serving.

Nutritional Info: Calories: 220 | Fat: 12g | Carbs: 20g | Protein: 9g

Tip: Feel free to customize the breakfast hash with your favorite vegetables or add cooked sausage or bacon for extra flavor.

Prep: 15 mins | Cook: 8 mins | Serves: 6

Ingredients:

- 200g plain flour and 2 tsp baking powder

- 100g granulated sugar and 1/4 tsp ground nutmeg

- 1/2 tsp ground cinnamon and 60ml vegetable oil

- Pinch of salt and 1 large egg

- 120ml milk and 1 tsp vanilla extract

For the Cinnamon Sugar Coating:

- 50g granulated sugar and 1 tsp ground cinnamon

- 50g unsalted butter, melted

Instructions:

1. Preheat your Air Fryer to 350°F using the Bake function.

2. In a large bowl, whisk together the plain flour, granulated sugar, baking powder, ground cinnamon, ground nutmeg, and salt.

3. In another bowl, mix together the milk, vegetable oil, egg, and vanilla extract until well combined.

4. Pour the wet ingredients into the dry ingredients and stir.

5. Spoon the batter into a greased donut pan, filling each cavity about 2/3 full.

6. Place the donut pan in the air fryer basket and air fry for 6-8 minutes until the donuts are golden brown and cooked through.

7. While the donuts are still warm, dip each one into the melted butter, then roll them in the cinnamon sugar coating until evenly coated.

8. Serve the cinnamon sugar donuts warm.

Nutritional Info: Calories: 280 | Fat: 12g | Carbs: 38g | Protein: 3g

Tip: Enjoy these cinnamon sugar donuts as a special treat for breakfast or brunch.

Prep: 15 mins | Cook: 10 mins | Serves: 4

Ingredients:

- 4 large eggs and 60ml milk

- Salt and pepper to taste

- 4 large spring roll wrappers

- 100g cooked ham, thinly sliced

- 100g shredded cheddar cheese

- Vegetable oil for brushing

Instructions:

1. Preheat your Instant Vortex Plus Dual Air Fryer to 375°F using the Air Fry function.

2. In a bowl, whisk together the eggs, milk, salt, and pepper until well combined.

3. Heat a skillet over medium heat and scramble the eggs until just set. Remove from heat.

4. Lay a spring roll wrapper flat on a clean surface.

5. Place a portion of scrambled eggs, sliced ham, and shredded cheddar cheese in the center of the wrapper.

6. Fold the sides of the wrapper over the filling, then roll it up tightly, sealing the edges with water.

7. Brush the outside of each egg roll with vegetable oil.

8. Place the egg rolls in the air fryer basket seam side down.

9. Air fry the egg rolls for 8-10 minutes until they are crispy.

10. Once done, remove the egg rolls from the air fryer and let them cool slightly before serving.

Nutritional Info: Calories: 320 | Fat: 16g | Carbs: 24g | Protein: 20g

Tip: Serve these breakfast egg rolls with your favorite dipping sauce, such as ketchup or sriracha mayo.

CHOCOLATE CHIP PANCAKES

Prep: 10 mins | Cook: 10 mins | Serves: 4

Ingredients:

- 200g self-raising flour
- 2 tbsp granulated sugar
- 1 tsp baking powder and Pinch of salt
- 240ml milk and 1 large egg
- 2 tbsp unsalted butter, melted
- 100g chocolate chips
- Maple syrup for serving

Instructions:

1. Preheat your Instant Vortex Plus Dual Air Fryer to 375°F using the Bake function.

2. In a large bowl, whisk together the self-raising flour, granulated sugar, baking powder, and salt.

3. In another bowl, mix together the milk, egg, and melted unsalted butter until well combined.

4. Pour the wet ingredients into the dry ingredients and stir.

5. Gently fold in the chocolate chips.

6. Grease the air fryer basket with a little butter or oil.

7. Pour small ladlefuls of the pancake batter into the air fryer basket, leaving space between each one.

8. Air fry the pancakes for 5 minutes, then flip them over and air fry for an additional 3-5 minutes until they are golden brown and cooked through.

9. Once done, remove the pancakes from the air fryer and serve hot with maple syrup.

Nutritional Info: Calories: 350 | Fat: 12g | Carbs: 52g | Protein: 8g

Tip: Feel free to add sliced bananas or chopped nuts to the pancake batter for extra flavor.

APPLE CINNAMON OATMEAL CUPS

Prep: 15 mins | Cook: 20 mins | Serves: 6

Ingredients:

- 2 large apples, peeled and grated

- 120g rolled oats

- 60g plain flour and Pinch of salt

- 2 tbsp brown sugar

- 1 tsp ground cinnamon

- 240ml milk and 1 tsp vanilla extract

- 1 large egg

Instructions:

1. Preheat your Instant Vortex Plus Dual Air Fryer to 350°F using the Bake function.

2. In a large bowl, combine the grated apples, rolled oats, plain flour, brown sugar, ground cinnamon, and salt.

3. In another bowl, whisk together the milk, egg, and vanilla extract until well combined.

4. Pour the wet ingredients into the dry ingredients and mix until just combined.

5. Grease a muffin tin or line it with paper liners.

6. Spoon the oatmeal mixture into the muffin cups, filling each one to the top.

7. Place the muffin tin in the air fryer basket and air fry for 18-20 minutes until the oatmeal cups are set and golden brown on top.

8. Once done, remove the oatmeal cups from the air fryer and let them cool slightly before serving.

Nutritional Info: Calories: 180 | Fat: 4g | Carbs: 32g | Protein: 5g

Tip: These apple cinnamon oatmeal cups can be enjoyed warm or cold, and they make a great grab-and-go breakfast option.

BREAKFAST PIZZA WITH EGGS AND BACON

Prep: 15 mins | Cook: 12 mins | Serves: 4

Ingredients:

- 1 pre-made pizza dough
- 120ml pizza sauce
- 100g shredded mozzarella cheese
- 4 slices of cooked bacon, crumbled
- 4 large eggs
- Salt and pepper to taste
- Chopped fresh parsley for garnish

Instructions:

1. Preheat your Instant Vortex Plus Dual Air Fryer to 375°F using the Bake function.

2. Roll out the pizza dough on a floured surface to fit the size of your air fryer basket.

3. Transfer the rolled-out dough to the greased air fryer basket.

4. Spread the pizza sauce evenly over the dough, leaving a border around the edges.

5. Sprinkle the shredded mozzarella cheese over the pizza sauce.

6. Scatter the crumbled bacon evenly over the cheese.

7. Carefully crack an egg onto each quarter of the pizza.

8. Season the eggs with salt and pepper to taste.

9. Air fry the breakfast pizza for 10-12 minutes until the crust is golden brown and the eggs are set.

10. Once done, remove the breakfast pizza from the air fryer and garnish with chopped fresh parsley before serving.

Nutritional Info: Calories: 380 | Fat: 20g | Carbs: 28g | Protein: 22g

Tip: Feel free to customize the breakfast pizza with your favorite toppings such as bell peppers, mushrooms, or sausage.

Prep: 10 mins | Cook: 10 mins | Serves: 4

Ingredients:

- 4 English muffins, split
- 4 cooked sausage patties
- 4 large eggs
- 4 slices of cheese
- Butter for spreading

Instructions:

1. Preheat your Instant Vortex Plus Dual Air Fryer to 375°F using the Air Fry function.

2. Place the split English muffins in the air fryer basket, cut side up.

3. Air fry the English muffins for 3-5 minutes until they are toasted and golden brown.

4. While the English muffins are toasting, place the cooked sausage patties in the air fryer basket.

5. Air fry the sausage patties for 5-7 minutes until they are heated through.

6. Once the English muffins and sausage patties are done, remove them from the air fryer and set aside.

7. Crack an egg into each quarter of the air fryer basket.

8. Air fry the eggs for 4-6 minutes until the whites are set but the yolks are still runny.

9. Once the eggs are cooked, assemble the breakfast sandwiches by placing a sausage patty, a slice of cheese, and a fried egg between each English muffin half.

10. Serve the sausage and egg breakfast sandwiches immediately.

Nutritional Info: Calories: 420 | Fat: 24g | Carbs: 30g | Protein: 22g

Tip: You can add a slice of cooked bacon or avocado slices to the breakfast sandwiches for extra flavor.

Prep: 15 mins | Cook: 20 mins | Serves: 4

Ingredients:

- 400g frozen hash browns, thawed

- 60g shredded cheddar cheese

- 4 large eggs

- Salt and pepper to taste

- Chopped fresh chives for garnish

Instructions:

1. Preheat your Instant Vortex Plus Dual Air Fryer to 375°F using the Air Fry function.

2. In a bowl, combine the thawed hash browns and shredded cheddar cheese.

3. Grease 4 cups of a muffin tin and divide the hash brown mixture evenly among the cups.

4. Use your fingers to press the hash browns into the bottom and up the sides of each cup to form nests.

5. Place the muffin tin in the air fryer basket and air fry for 10-12 minutes until the hash browns are golden brown and crispy.

6. Once the hash browns are cooked, crack an egg into each nest.

7. Season the eggs with salt and pepper to taste.

8. Air fry the egg nests for an additional 8-10 minutes until the egg whites are set but the yolks are still runny.

9. Once done, remove the egg nests from the air fryer and garnish with chopped fresh chives before serving.

Nutritional Info: Calories: 280 | Fat: 16g | Carbs: 20g | Protein: 14g

Tip: These hash brown egg nests are perfect for brunch or a hearty breakfast. Serve them with a side of salsa or avocado slices for extra flavor.

CRISPY MOZZARELLA STICKS WITH MARINARA SAUCE

Prep: 15 mins | Cook: 10 mins | Serves: 4

Ingredients:

- 200g mozzarella cheese, cut into sticks

- 100g plain flour

- 2 large eggs, beaten

- 100g breadcrumbs

- 1 tsp Italian seasoning

- 200ml marinara sauce

Instructions:

1. Preheat your Instant Vortex Plus Dual Air Fryer to 200°C using the Air Fry function.

2. Dip each mozzarella stick into the flour, then the beaten eggs, and finally coat with breadcrumbs mixed with Italian seasoning.

3. Place the coated mozzarella sticks in the air fryer basket in a single layer.

4. Air fry for 8-10 minutes until golden and crispy, flipping halfway through.

5. Serve hot with marinara sauce for dipping.

Nutritional Info (per serving): Calories: 280 | Fat: 15g | Carbs: 20g | Protein: 14g

CRISPY BUFFALO CAULIFLOWER BITES

Prep: 10 mins | Cook: 20 mins | Serves: 4

Ingredients:

- 1 medium cauliflower, cut into florets

- 100g plain flour

- 100ml milk

- 100g breadcrumbs

- 1 tsp garlic powder

- 100ml buffalo sauce

Instructions:

1. Preheat your Instant Vortex Plus Dual Air Fryer to 180°C using the Air Fry function.

2. In a bowl, whisk together flour and milk to create a batter.

3. Dip each cauliflower floret into the batter, then coat with breadcrumbs mixed with garlic powder.

4. Place the coated cauliflower florets in the air fryer basket in a single layer.

5. Air fry for 15-20 minutes until crispy, shaking halfway through.

6. Toss the cooked cauliflower in buffalo sauce until evenly coated.

7. Serve hot with your favorite dipping sauce.

Nutritional Info (per serving): Calories: 180 | Fat: 4g | Carbs: 30g | Protein: 7g

Prep: 15 mins | Cook: 20 mins | Serves: 4

Ingredients:

- 4 large potatoes, thinly sliced

- 2 tbsp olive oil

- Salt and pepper to taste

- For the dipping sauce:

- 100g Greek yogurt

- 1 tbsp chopped chives

- 1 tsp garlic powder

- Salt and pepper to taste

Instructions:

1. Preheat your Instant Vortex Plus Dual Air Fryer to 200°C using the Air Fry function.

2. In a bowl, toss the potato slices with olive oil, salt, and pepper until evenly coated.

3. Arrange the potato slices in a single layer in the air fryer basket.

4. Air fry for 15-20 minutes until golden and crispy, shaking halfway through.

5. Meanwhile, mix together Greek yogurt, chives, garlic powder, salt, and pepper to make the dipping sauce.

6. Serve the hot potato chips with the prepared dipping sauce.

Nutritional Info (per serving): Calories: 220 | Fat: 8g | Carbs: 32g | Protein: 5g

STUFFED JALAPEÑO POPPERS WITH CREAM CHEESE

Prep: 20 mins | Cook: 12 mins | Serves: 4

Ingredients:

- 8 large jalapeño peppers

- 100g cream cheese

- 50g grated cheddar cheese

- 50g breadcrumbs

- 1 tsp paprika

- Salt and pepper to taste

Instructions:

1. Preheat your Instant Vortex Plus Dual Air Fryer to 180°C using the Air Fry function.

2. Cut the jalapeño peppers in half lengthwise and remove the seeds.

3. In a bowl, mix together cream cheese, cheddar cheese, breadcrumbs, paprika, salt, and pepper.

4. Stuff each jalapeño half with the cream cheese mixture.

5. Arrange the stuffed jalapeños in the air fryer basket.

6. Air fry for 10-12 minutes until the peppers are tender and the filling is golden and bubbly.

7. Serve hot as a delicious appetizer.

Nutritional Info (per serving): Calories: 150 | Fat: 10g | Carbs: 10g | Protein: 6g

Prep: 15 mins | Cook: 10 mins | Serves: 4

Ingredients:

- 2 large onions, cut into rings
- 100g plain flour
- 2 large eggs, beaten
- 100g breadcrumbs
- 1 tsp smoked paprika
- Salt and pepper to taste
- For the spicy dipping sauce:
- 100g mayonnaise
- 1 tbsp hot sauce
- 1 tsp honey

Instructions:

1. Preheat your Instant Vortex Plus Dual Air Fryer to 200°C using the Air Fry function.

2. Dip each onion ring into the flour, then the beaten eggs, and finally coat with breadcrumbs mixed with smoked paprika, salt, and pepper.

3. Place the coated onion rings in the air fryer basket in a single layer.

4. Air fry for 8-10 minutes until golden and crispy, flipping halfway through.

5. Meanwhile, mix together mayonnaise, hot sauce, and honey to make the spicy dipping sauce.

6. Serve the hot crispy onion rings with the prepared spicy dipping sauce.

Nutritional Info (per serving): Calories: 280 | Fat: 15g | Carbs: 30g | Protein: 6g

BACON-WRAPPED DATES WITH GOAT CHEESE

Prep: 15 mins | Cook: 15 mins | Serves: 4

Ingredients:

- 16 Medjool dates, pitted
- 100g soft goat cheese
- 8 slices of bacon, cut in half
- Toothpicks

Instructions:

1. Preheat your Instant Vortex Plus Dual Air Fryer to 180°C using the Air Fry function.
2. Stuff each date with a teaspoon of goat cheese.
3. Wrap each stuffed date with a half-slice of bacon and secure with a toothpick.
4. Arrange the bacon-wrapped dates in the air fryer basket.
5. Air fry for 12-15 minutes until the bacon is crispy and golden.
6. Serve hot as a delicious appetizer or snack.

Nutritional Info (per serving): Calories: 220 | Fat: 12g | Carbs: 25g | Protein: 7g

Prep: 20 mins | Cook: 15 mins | Serves: 4

Ingredients:

- 1 can (400g) refrigerated pizza dough

- 2 tbsp butter, melted

- 2 cloves garlic, minced

- 50g grated Parmesan cheese

- 1 tsp dried parsley

- Salt to taste

Instructions:

1. Preheat your Instant Vortex Plus Dual Air Fryer to 180°C using the Air Fry function.

2. Roll out the pizza dough on a lightly floured surface and cut into breadstick shapes.

3. In a small bowl, mix together melted butter, minced garlic, grated Parmesan cheese, dried parsley, and salt.

4. Brush the butter mixture over the breadsticks.

5. Arrange the breadsticks in the air fryer basket.

6. Air fry for 12-15 minutes until golden and crispy.

7. Serve hot as a tasty appetizer or side dish.

Nutritional Info (per serving): Calories: 240 | Fat: 10g | Carbs: 30g | Protein: 6g

CRISPY ASIAN SPRING ROLLS WITH SWEET CHILI SAUCE

Prep: 25 mins | Cook: 15 mins | Serves: 4

Ingredients:

- 8 spring roll wrappers
- 100g cooked vermicelli noodles
- 1 carrot, julienned
- 1 red bell pepper, thinly sliced
- 50g cabbage, shredded
- 50g bean sprouts
- 2 spring onions, thinly sliced
- 1 tbsp soy sauce
- 1 tsp sesame oil
- 1 tsp grated ginger
- Sweet chili sauce, for dipping

Instructions:

1.   In a bowl, mix together cooked vermicelli noodles, julienned carrot, sliced bell pepper, shredded cabbage, bean sprouts, sliced spring onions, soy sauce, sesame oil, and grated ginger.

2.   Place a spoonful of the filling onto each spring roll wrapper and fold according to package instructions.

3.   Preheat your Instant Vortex Plus Dual Air Fryer to 180°C using the Air Fry function.

4.   Lightly brush the spring rolls with oil and place them in the air fryer basket.

5.   Air fry for 12-15 minutes until golden and crispy.

6.   Serve hot with sweet chili sauce for dipping.

Nutritional Info (per serving): Calories: 180 | Fat: 5g | Carbs: 28g | Protein: 4g

Prep: 15 mins | Cook: 15 mins | Serves: 4

Ingredients:

- 200g cream cheese

- 100g sour cream

- 100g mayonnaise

- 50g grated Parmesan cheese

- 1 clove garlic, minced

- 100g frozen chopped spinach, thawed and drained

- 200g canned artichoke hearts, drained and chopped

- Salt and pepper to taste

- Tortilla chips, for serving

Instructions:

1. In a bowl, mix together cream cheese, sour cream, mayonnaise, grated Parmesan cheese, minced garlic, chopped spinach, and chopped artichoke hearts.

2. Season with salt and pepper to taste.

3. Preheat your Instant Vortex Plus Dual Air Fryer to 180°C using the Air Fry function.

4. Transfer the spinach and artichoke dip to an oven-safe dish.

5. Place the dish in the air fryer basket.

6. Air fry for 12-15 minutes until bubbly and golden on top.

7. Serve hot with tortilla chips for dipping.

Nutritional Info (per serving): Calories: 280 | Fat: 25g | Carbs: 8g | Protein: 6g

Prep: 15 mins | Cook: 20 mins | Serves: 4

Ingredients:

- 2 large sweet potatoes, cut into fries
- 2 tbsp olive oil
- 1 tsp paprika
- 1 tsp garlic powder
- Salt and pepper to taste

For the sriracha aioli:

- 100g mayonnaise
- 1 tbsp sriracha sauce
- 1 tsp lemon juice
- 1 clove garlic, minced

Instructions:

1.   In a bowl, toss sweet potato fries with olive oil, paprika, garlic powder, salt, and pepper until evenly coated.

2.   Preheat your Instant Vortex Plus Dual Air Fryer to 200°C using the Air Fry function.

3.   Arrange the sweet potato fries in a single layer in the air fryer basket.

4.   Air fry for 15-20 minutes until crispy and golden, shaking halfway through.

5.   Meanwhile, prepare the sriracha aioli by mixing together mayonnaise, sriracha sauce, lemon juice, and minced garlic.

6.   Serve the hot sweet potato fries with the prepared sriracha aioli for dipping.

Nutritional Info (per serving): Calories: 220 | Fat: 10g | Carbs: 30g | Protein: 3g

Prep: 20 mins | Cook: 15 mins | Serves: 4

Ingredients:

- 250g minced beef
- 1 small onion, finely chopped
- 1 clove garlic, minced
- 50g breadcrumbs
- 1 egg
- Salt and pepper to taste
- For the BBQ glaze:
- 50ml BBQ sauce
- 1 tbsp honey
- 1 tsp Worcestershire sauce

Instructions:

1. In a bowl, mix together minced beef, chopped onion, minced garlic, breadcrumbs, egg, salt, and pepper until well combined.

2. Shape the mixture into miniature meatballs.

3. Preheat your Instant Vortex Plus Dual Air Fryer to 180°C using the Air Fry function.

4. Arrange the meatballs in a single layer in the air fryer basket.

5. Air fry for 12-15 minutes until cooked through and lightly browned.

6. Meanwhile, prepare the BBQ glaze by mixing together BBQ sauce, honey, and Worcestershire sauce.

7. Once cooked, brush the meatballs with the BBQ glaze.

8. Serve hot as a delicious appetizer or snack.

Nutritional Info (per serving): Calories: 220 | Fat: 10g | Carbs: 15g | Protein: 15g

Prep: 20 mins | Cook: 10 mins | Serves: 4

Ingredients:

- 2 ripe avocados, mashed

- 1 small red onion, finely chopped

- 1 small tomato, diced

- 2 tbsp chopped cilantro

- Juice of 1 lime

- Salt and pepper to taste

- 8 egg roll wrappers

- Oil for brushing

For the cilantro lime dip:

- 100g sour cream

- Juice of 1 lime

- 1 tbsp chopped cilantro

- Salt to taste

Instructions:

1. In a bowl, mix together mashed avocados, chopped red onion, diced tomato, chopped cilantro, lime juice, salt, and pepper.

2. Place a spoonful of the avocado mixture onto each egg roll wrapper.

3. Roll up the wrappers, folding in the sides, and sealing with water.

4. Preheat your Instant Vortex Plus Dual Air Fryer to 200°C using the Air Fry function.

5. Brush the avocado egg rolls with oil and place them in the air fryer basket.

6. Air fry for 8-10 minutes until golden and crispy.

7. Meanwhile, prepare the cilantro lime dip by mixing together sour cream, lime juice, chopped cilantro, and salt.

8. Serve the hot avocado egg rolls with the cilantro lime dip.

Nutritional Info (per serving): Calories: 250 | Fat: 12g | Carbs: 30g | Protein: 5g

Prep: 20 mins | Cook: 10 mins | Serves: 4

Ingredients:

- 200g large shrimp, peeled and deveined
- 100g shredded coconut
- 50g breadcrumbs
- 1 egg, beaten
- Salt and pepper to taste
- Oil for spraying

For the mango salsa:

- 1 ripe mango, diced
- 1/2 red onion, finely chopped
- 1/2 red bell pepper, diced
- Juice of 1 lime
- 2 tbsp chopped cilantro
- Salt and pepper to taste

Instructions:

1. In a bowl, mix together shredded coconut and breadcrumbs.

2. Dip each shrimp into beaten egg, then coat with the coconut breadcrumb mixture.

3. Preheat your Instant Vortex Plus Dual Air Fryer to 200°C using the Air Fry function.

4. Arrange the coated shrimp in a single layer in the air fryer basket.

5. Lightly spray the shrimp with oil.

6. Air fry for 8-10 minutes until golden and crispy.

7. Meanwhile, prepare the mango salsa by mixing together diced mango, chopped red onion, diced red bell pepper, lime juice, chopped cilantro, salt, and pepper.

8. Serve the hot coconut shrimp with the mango salsa.

Nutritional Info (per serving): Calories: 280 | Fat: 15g | Carbs: 20g | Protein: 15g

Prep: 10 mins | Cook: 15 mins | Serves: 4

Ingredients:

- 400g canned chickpeas, drained and rinsed
- 2 tbsp olive oil
- 1 tsp smoked paprika
- 1 tsp cumin
- 1/2 tsp garlic powder
- Salt and pepper to taste
- 50g mixed nuts

Instructions:

1.   In a bowl, toss together chickpeas, olive oil, smoked paprika, cumin, garlic powder, salt, and pepper until evenly coated.

2.   Preheat your Instant Vortex Plus Dual Air Fryer to 200°C using the Air Fry function.

3.   Arrange the seasoned chickpeas and mixed nuts in a single layer in the air fryer basket.

4.   Air fry for 12-15 minutes until crispy and golden, shaking halfway through.

5.   Serve the crispy chickpea snack mix as a delicious and healthy snack.

Nutritional Info (per serving): Calories: 220 | Fat: 10g | Carbs: 25g | Protein: 8g

BAKED MINIATURE EMPANADAS WITH BEEF FILLING

Prep: 30 mins | Cook: 15 mins | Serves: 4

Ingredients:

- 1 tbsp olive oil

- 1 small onion, finely chopped

- 1 clove garlic, minced

- 200g minced beef

- 1 tsp ground cumin

- 1/2 tsp smoked paprika

- Salt and pepper to taste

- 8 mini empanada wrappers

- 1 egg, beaten

- For serving: salsa or chimichurri sauce

Instructions:

1. In a pan, heat olive oil over medium heat and sauté chopped onion and minced garlic until softened.

2. Add minced beef to the pan and cook until browned.

3. Stir in ground cumin, smoked paprika, salt, and pepper. Remove from heat and let cool slightly.

4. Preheat your Instant Vortex Plus Dual Air Fryer to 180°C using the Air Fry function.

5. Spoon a tablespoon of the beef filling onto each empanada wrapper.

6. Fold the wrappers over the filling, sealing the edges with beaten egg.

7. Arrange the empanadas in a single layer in the air fryer basket.

8. Air fry for 12-15 minutes until golden and crispy.

9. Serve the hot miniature empanadas with salsa or chimichurri sauce.

Nutritional Info (per serving): Calories: 280 | Fat: 15g | Carbs: 20g | Protein: 12g

CHAPTER 3: FAMILY FAVORITES RECIPES

CLASSIC CHICKEN WINGS WITH BUFFALO SAUCE

Prep: 10 mins | Cook: 25 mins | Serves: 4

Ingredients:

- 1 kg chicken wings
- 2 tbsp olive oil
- Salt and pepper to taste
- 100g butter
- 120ml hot sauce
- 1 tbsp Worcestershire sauce
- 1 tsp garlic powder

Instructions:

1. Preheat the Instant Vortex Plus Dual Air Fryer to 180°C using the Air Fry function.

2. In a bowl, toss the chicken wings with olive oil, salt, and pepper until evenly coated.

3. Place the seasoned wings in the air fryer basket in a single layer. Cook for 25 minutes, flipping halfway through.

4. While the wings are cooking, melt the butter in a saucepan over low heat. Stir in the hot sauce, Worcestershire sauce, and garlic powder.

5. Once the wings are crispy and golden brown, remove them from the air fryer and toss them in the buffalo sauce until coated.

6. Serve hot with celery sticks and blue cheese dressing.

Nutritional Info (per serving): Calories: 350 | Fat: 25g | Carbs: 3g | Protein: 28g

Tricky Technique: Ensure to flip the wings halfway through cooking for even crisping.

Prep: 15 mins | Cook: 12 mins | Serves: 6

Ingredients:

- 1 pre-made pizza dough
- 2 tbsp butter, melted
- 2 cloves garlic, minced
- 1/2 tsp dried parsley
- 100g mozzarella cheese, shredded
- 50g Parmesan cheese, grated

Instructions:

1. Preheat the Instant Vortex Plus Dual Air Fryer to 180°C using the Bake function.

2. Roll out the pizza dough on a floured surface into a rectangle.

3. In a small bowl, mix together the melted butter, minced garlic, and dried parsley.

4. Brush the garlic butter mixture evenly over the pizza dough.

5. Sprinkle the mozzarella cheese and Parmesan cheese over the dough.

6. Cut the dough into breadsticks and place them in the air fryer basket.

7. Bake for 12 minutes until the breadsticks are golden brown and crispy.

8. Serve warm with marinara sauce for dipping.

Nutritional Info (per serving): Calories: 220 | Fat: 10g | Carbs: 25g | Protein: 9g

Tricky Technique: Ensure to brush the garlic butter mixture evenly over the dough to infuse flavor into every bite.

Prep: 15 mins | Cook: 20 mins | Serves: 4

Ingredients:

- 4 boneless, skinless chicken breasts
- 100g breadcrumbs
- 50g grated Parmesan cheese
- 1 tsp Italian seasoning
- Salt and pepper to taste
- 120ml marinara sauce and 2 eggs, beaten
- 100g mozzarella cheese, shredded
- Fresh basil leaves for garnish

Instructions:

1. Preheat the Air Fryer to 200°C using the Air Fry function.

2. In a shallow dish, combine the breadcrumbs, Parmesan cheese, Italian seasoning, salt, and pepper.

3. Dip each chicken breast into the beaten eggs, then coat evenly with the breadcrumb mixture.

4. Place the breaded chicken breasts in the air fryer basket in a single layer.

5. Air fry for 20 minutes, flipping halfway through, until the chicken is golden brown and cooked through.

6. Spoon marinara sauce over each chicken breast and sprinkle with shredded mozzarella cheese.

7. Air fry for an additional 2-3 minutes until the cheese is melted and bubbly.

8. Garnish with fresh basil leaves before serving.

Nutritional Info (per serving): Calories: 350 | Fat: 12g | Carbs: 15g | Protein: 40g

Tricky Technique: Ensure the chicken breasts are evenly coated with the breadcrumb mixture for maximum crispiness.

Prep: 20 mins | Cook: 12 mins | Serves: 4

Ingredients:

- 2 chicken breasts, cut into bite-sized pieces
- 100g plain flour and 1 tsp paprika
- 2 eggs, beaten
- 150g breadcrumbs and Salt and pepper to taste
- Cooking spray and 4 tbsp honey
- 2 tbsp Dijon mustard

Instructions:

1. Preheat the Air Fryer to 200°C using the Air Fry function.

2. Place the flour, beaten eggs, and breadcrumbs mixed with paprika in separate shallow dishes.

3. Season the chicken pieces with salt and pepper.

4. Dip each chicken piece first in the flour, then the beaten eggs, and finally coat evenly with breadcrumbs.

5. Place the breaded chicken nuggets in a single layer in the air fryer basket.

6. Lightly spray the nuggets with cooking spray.

7. Air fry for 12 minutes, flipping halfway through, until the nuggets are golden brown and cooked through.

8. In a small bowl, mix together the honey and Dijon mustard to make the dip.

9. Serve the crispy chicken nuggets with the honey mustard dip on the side.

Nutritional Info (per serving): Calories: 320 | Fat: 8g | Carbs: 40g | Protein: 25g

Tricky Technique: Ensure the chicken nuggets are spaced apart in the air fryer basket for even cooking.

Prep: 10 mins | Cook: 25 mins | Serves: 4

Ingredients:

- 8 chicken drumsticks

- 120ml BBQ sauce

- 1 tbsp olive oil

- 1 tsp smoked paprika

- Salt and pepper to taste

- Fresh parsley for garnish

Instructions:

1. Preheat the Instant Vortex Plus Dual Air Fryer to 180°C using the Air Fry function.

2. In a bowl, mix together the BBQ sauce, olive oil, smoked paprika, salt, and pepper.

3. Brush the BBQ sauce mixture evenly over the chicken drumsticks.

4. Place the drumsticks in the air fryer basket in a single layer.

5. Air fry for 25 minutes, flipping halfway through, until the chicken is cooked through and crispy.

6. Garnish with fresh parsley before serving.

Nutritional Info (per serving): Calories: 280 | Fat: 10g | Carbs: 15g | Protein: 30g

Tricky Technique: Ensure the chicken drumsticks are coated evenly with the BBQ sauce mixture for maximum flavor.

LOADED POTATO SKINS WITH BACON AND CHEESE

Prep: 20 mins | Cook: 25 mins | Serves: 4

Ingredients:

- 4 large russet potatoes

- 4 slices bacon, cooked and crumbled

- 100g Cheddar cheese, shredded

- 2 spring onions, thinly sliced

- Salt and pepper to taste

- Sour cream for serving

Instructions:

1.   Preheat the Instant Vortex Plus Dual Air Fryer to 200°C using the Air Fry function.

2.   Scrub the potatoes clean and pat dry. Pierce the potatoes several times with a fork.

3.   Place the potatoes in the air fryer basket and air fry for 25 minutes, until tender.

4.   Allow the potatoes to cool slightly, then cut them in half lengthwise.

5.   Scoop out the flesh from each potato half, leaving about 1/4 inch of flesh attached to the skin.

6.   Place the potato skins back in the air fryer basket, skin side down.

7.   Season the potato skins with salt and pepper, then sprinkle with shredded Cheddar cheese and crumbled bacon.

8.   Air fry for an additional 5 minutes, until the cheese is melted and bubbly.

9.   Garnish with sliced spring onions and serve with sour cream on the side.

Nutritional Info (per serving): Calories: 300 | Fat: 15g | Carbs: 30g | Protein: 12g

Tricky Technique: Ensure to leave a thin layer of flesh attached to the potato skins to maintain their structure.

Prep: 20 mins | Cook: 15 mins | Serves: 4

Ingredients:

- 4 boneless, skinless chicken breasts
- 100g plain flour
- 2 eggs, beaten
- 150g breadcrumbs
- 1 tsp paprika and 120ml sour cream
- Salt and pepper to taste
- 8 small flour tortillas
- 1 avocado, peeled and pitted
- Juice of 1 lime
- 2 tbsp fresh coriander, chopped
- 1 tomato, diced
- Shredded lettuce for serving

Instructions:

1. Preheat the Instant Vortex Plus Dual Air Fryer to 200°C using the Air Fry function.

2. Season the chicken breasts with salt and pepper.

3. Place the flour, beaten eggs, and breadcrumbs mixed with paprika in separate shallow dishes.

4. Dredge each chicken breast first in the flour, then the beaten eggs, and finally coat evenly with breadcrumbs.

5. Place the breaded chicken breasts in the air fryer basket in a single layer.

6. Air fry for 15 minutes, flipping halfway through, until the chicken is golden brown and cooked through.

7. While the chicken is cooking, prepare the avocado crema by blending together the avocado, sour cream, lime juice, and fresh coriander until smooth. Season with salt and pepper to taste.

8. Once the chicken is cooked, slice it into strips.

9. Warm the flour tortillas in the air fryer for 1-2 minutes.

10. To assemble the tacos, place a few slices of crispy chicken on each tortilla. Top with diced tomato, shredded lettuce, and a dollop of avocado crema.

11. Serve immediately with lime wedges on the side.

Nutritional Info (per serving): Calories: 350 | Fat: 12g | Carbs: 35g | Protein: 25g

Tricky Technique: Ensure the chicken breasts are evenly coated with the breadcrumb mixture for maximum crispiness.

BEEF AND CHEESE QUESADILLAS

Prep: 10 mins | Cook: 10 mins | Serves: 4

Ingredients:

- 4 large flour tortillas
- 200g cooked beef mince
- 100g Cheddar cheese, shredded
- 1 red pepper, thinly sliced
- 1 green pepper, thinly sliced
- 1 onion, thinly sliced
- Salt and pepper to taste
- Guacamole and salsa for serving

Instructions:

1. Preheat the Instant Vortex Plus Dual Air Fryer to 180°C using the Air Fry function.

2. Place a flour tortilla on a flat surface and sprinkle half of it with shredded Cheddar cheese.

3. Top the cheese with cooked beef mince, sliced peppers, and onions. Season with salt and pepper.

4. Fold the tortilla in half to enclose the filling.

5. Repeat with the remaining tortillas and filling ingredients.

6. Place the quesadillas in the air fryer basket in a single layer.

7. Air fry for 5 minutes, then flip the quesadillas and air fry for an additional 5 minutes until golden brown and crispy.

8. Remove the quesadillas from the air fryer and cut each one into wedges.

9. Serve hot with guacamole and salsa on the side.

Nutritional Info (per serving): Calories: 320 | Fat: 15g | Carbs: 30g | Protein: 20g

Tricky Technique: Ensure to flip the quesadillas halfway through cooking for even crisping.

Prep: 20 mins | Cook: 25 mins | Serves: 4

Ingredients:

- 4 large bell peppers, halved and seeds removed

- 200g cooked rice

- 100g grated Cheddar cheese

- 1 onion, diced

- 2 cloves garlic, minced

- 1 carrot, grated

- 1 courgette, grated

- 120ml vegetable stock

- 1 tsp dried mixed herbs

- Salt and pepper to taste

- Fresh parsley for garnish

Instructions:

1. Preheat the Instant Vortex Plus Dual Air Fryer to 180°C using the Air Fry function.

2. In a large bowl, mix together the cooked rice, grated Cheddar cheese, diced onion, minced garlic, grated carrot, grated courgette, vegetable stock, dried mixed herbs, salt, and pepper.

3. Spoon the rice mixture evenly into each bell pepper half.

4. Place the stuffed bell peppers in the air fryer basket in a single layer.

5. Air fry for 25 minutes, until the peppers are tender and the filling is heated through.

6. Garnish with fresh parsley before serving.

Nutritional Info (per serving): Calories: 280 | Fat: 10g | Carbs: 35g | Protein: 10g

Tricky Technique: Ensure the bell peppers are evenly stuffed and packed tightly to prevent the filling from falling out during cooking.

Prep: 20 mins | Cook: 15 mins | Serves: 4

Ingredients:

- 400g lean minced beef

- 1 egg, beaten

- 50g breadcrumbs

- 1 tsp dried oregano

- Salt and pepper to taste

- 8 small mozzarella balls and 120ml marinara sauce

- Fresh basil leaves for garnish

Instructions:

1. Preheat the Air Fryer to 200°C using the Air Fry function.

2. In a bowl, mix together the minced beef, beaten egg, breadcrumbs, dried oregano, salt, and pepper until well combined.

3. Take a small portion of the beef mixture and flatten it in the palm of your hand.

4. Place a mozzarella ball in the center of the beef mixture and wrap the beef around it, forming a meatball.

5. Repeat with the remaining beef mixture and mozzarella balls.

6. Place the meatballs in the air fryer basket in a single layer.

7. Air fry for 15 minutes, until the meatballs are golden brown and cooked through.

8. Heat the marinara sauce in a saucepan over low heat.

9. Serve the crispy mozzarella-stuffed meatballs with marinara sauce and garnish with fresh basil leaves.

Nutritional Info (per serving): Calories: 320 | Fat: 15g | Carbs: 10g | Protein: 35g

Tricky Technique: Ensure to seal the beef mixture tightly around the mozzarella ball to prevent the cheese melting out during cooking.

LEMON HERB SALMON FILLETS

Prep: 10 mins | Cook: 15 mins | Serves: 4

Ingredients:

- 4 salmon fillets (about 150g each)

- 2 tablespoons olive oil

- 2 cloves garlic, minced

- 1 lemon, zest and juice

- 2 teaspoons chopped fresh dill

- Salt and pepper to taste

Instructions:

1. Preheat your Instant Vortex Plus Dual Air Fryer to 180°C using the Air Fry function.

2. In a small bowl, mix together olive oil, minced garlic, lemon zest, lemon juice, and chopped dill.

3. Season salmon fillets with salt and pepper, then brush with the lemon herb mixture.

4. Place salmon fillets in the air fryer basket and cook for 12-15 minutes until salmon is cooked through and flakes easily with a fork.

5. Serve hot, garnished with extra lemon slices if desired.

Nutritional Info: Calories: 280 | Fat: 18g | Carbs: 2g | Protein: 26g

SHRIMP SCAMPI WITH GARLIC BUTTER

Prep: 10 mins | Cook: 8 mins | Serves: 4

Ingredients:

- 500g large shrimp, peeled and deveined
- 4 tablespoons unsalted butter
- 4 cloves garlic, minced
- 2 tablespoons lemon juice
- 2 tablespoons chopped fresh parsley
- Salt and pepper to taste

Instructions:

1. Preheat your Instant Vortex Plus Dual Air Fryer to 200°C using the Air Fry function.

2. In a small microwave-safe bowl, melt butter and mix in minced garlic, lemon juice, chopped parsley, salt, and pepper.

3. Toss shrimp in the garlic butter mixture until evenly coated.

4. Place shrimp in the air fryer basket in a single layer and cook for 5-8 minutes until shrimp are pink and opaque.

5. Serve hot, garnished with additional parsley and lemon wedges.

Nutritional Info: Calories: 210 | Fat: 14g | Carbs: 2g | Protein: 18g

Prep: 15 mins | Cook: 20 mins | Serves: 4

Ingredients:

- 4 white fish fillets (such as cod or haddock), about 150g each

- 100g plain flour

- 1 teaspoon baking powder and 100g breadcrumbs

- 1 teaspoon salt and 120ml beer

- Cooking spray and 1 egg

- Salt and vinegar, to serve

Tartar Sauce:

- 150g mayonnaise and 1 tablespoon lemon juice

- 2 tablespoons chopped gherkins

- 1 tablespoon capers, chopped

- 1 tablespoon chopped fresh parsley

- Salt and pepper to taste

Instructions:

1. Preheat your Instant Vortex Plus Dual Air Fryer to 200°C using the Air Fry function.

2. In a shallow dish, mix together flour, baking powder, and salt.

3. In another bowl, beat the egg and beer together.

4. Dip each fish fillet into the flour mixture, then into the egg mixture, and finally coat with breadcrumbs.

5. Place the coated fish fillets in the air fryer basket, spray with cooking spray, and cook for 15-20 minutes until golden and crispy.

6. Meanwhile, prepare the tartar sauce by mixing together mayonnaise, chopped gherkins, capers, parsley, lemon juice, salt, and pepper.

7. Serve the crispy fish and chips with tartar sauce, salt, and vinegar.

Nutritional Info: (per serving, including tartar sauce) Calories: 450 | Fat: 25g | Carbs: 32g | Protein: 25g

Prep: 15 mins | Cook: 10 mins | Serves: 4

Ingredients:

- 500g large shrimp, peeled and deveined

- 100g shredded coconut

- 50g breadcrumbs and 1 teaspoon paprika

- 1 teaspoon garlic powder and 1 egg, beaten

- Salt and pepper to taste and Cooking spray

Mango Salsa:

- 1 ripe mango, diced

- 1/2 red onion, finely chopped and Juice of 1 lime

- 1 red chili, seeded and finely chopped

- 2 tablespoons chopped fresh cilantro and Salt to taste

Instructions:

1. Preheat your Instant Vortex Plus Dual Air Fryer to 200°C using the Air Fry function.

2. In one bowl, mix together shredded coconut, breadcrumbs, garlic powder, paprika, salt, and pepper.

3. Dip each shrimp in beaten egg, then coat with the coconut breadcrumb mixture.

4. Place the coated shrimp in the air fryer basket in a single layer, spray with cooking spray, and cook for 8-10 minutes until shrimp are golden and crispy.

5. While the shrimp are cooking, prepare the mango salsa by combining diced mango, chopped red onion, red chili, lime juice, cilantro, and salt in a bowl.

6. Serve the crispy coconut shrimp with mango salsa on the side.

Nutritional Info: (per serving, including mango salsa) Calories: 320 | Fat: 12g | Carbs: 30g | Protein: 24g

Prep: 10 mins | Cook: 12 mins | Serves: 4

Ingredients:

- 4 tilapia fillets, about 150g each
- 2 tablespoons olive oil
- 2 tablespoons Cajun seasoning
- 1 teaspoon paprika
- 1/2 teaspoon garlic powder
- 1/2 teaspoon onion powder
- Salt and pepper to taste
- Lemon wedges, for serving

Instructions:

1. Preheat your Instant Vortex Plus Dual Air Fryer to 190°C using the Air Fry function.

2. In a small bowl, mix together Cajun seasoning, paprika, garlic powder, onion powder, salt, and pepper.

3. Brush each tilapia fillet with olive oil and sprinkle with the Cajun seasoning mixture, coating both sides.

4. Place the seasoned tilapia fillets in the air fryer basket and cook for 10-12 minutes until fish is cooked through and flakes easily with a fork.

5. Serve hot, garnished with lemon wedges.

Nutritional Info: Calories: 180 | Fat: 9g | Carbs: 2g | Protein: 23g

Prep: 15 mins | Cook: 8 mins | Serves: 4

Ingredients:

- 500g large shrimp, peeled and deveined
- 2 tablespoons olive oil
- Zest of 1 lemon
- 2 teaspoons freshly ground black pepper
- 1 teaspoon garlic powder
- Salt to taste
- Lemon wedges, for serving

Instructions:

1. Preheat your Instant Vortex Plus Dual Air Fryer to 200°C using the Air Fry function.

2. In a bowl, toss shrimp with olive oil, lemon zest, black pepper, garlic powder, and salt.

3. Thread shrimp onto skewers, leaving space between each shrimp.

4. Place the shrimp skewers in the air fryer basket and cook for 6-8 minutes until shrimp are pink and cooked through.

5. Serve hot, garnished with lemon wedges.

Nutritional Info: Calories: 180 | Fat: 9g | Carbs: 2g | Protein: 24g

CRISPY CALAMARI RINGS WITH MARINARA SAUCE

Prep: 20 mins | Cook: 8 mins | Serves: 4

Ingredients:

- 500g calamari rings
- 100g plain flour
- 2 eggs, beaten
- 100g breadcrumbs
- 1 teaspoon garlic powder
- 1 teaspoon paprika
- Salt and pepper to taste AND Cooking spray

Marinara Sauce:

- 400g canned chopped tomatoes
- 2 cloves garlic, minced
- 1 tablespoon olive oil
- 1 teaspoon dried oregano
- Salt and pepper to taste
- Fresh basil leaves, for garnish

Instructions:

1. Preheat your Instant Vortex Plus Dual Air Fryer to 200°C using the Air Fry function.

2. In one shallow dish, place flour. In another dish, place beaten eggs. In a third dish, mix together breadcrumbs, garlic powder, paprika, salt, and pepper.

3. Dredge calamari rings in flour, dip in beaten eggs, then coat with breadcrumb mixture, pressing gently to adhere.

4. Place coated calamari rings in the air fryer basket in a single layer, spray with cooking spray, and cook for 6-8 minutes until golden and crispy.

5. While calamari is cooking, prepare the marinara sauce by heating olive oil in a saucepan, sautéing minced garlic until fragrant, then adding chopped tomatoes, dried oregano, salt, and pepper. Simmer for 5 minutes.

6. Serve crispy calamari rings hot with marinara sauce, garnished with fresh basil leaves.

Nutritional Info: (per serving, including marinara sauce) Calories: 320 | Fat: 8g | Carbs: 45g | Protein: 18g

Prep: 15 mins | Cook: 10 mins | Serves: 4

Ingredients:

- 4 mahi mahi fillets, about 150g each

- 2 tablespoons soy sauce

- 1 tablespoon honey

- 1 tablespoon sesame oil

- 1 tablespoon grated ginger

- 2 cloves garlic, minced

- 1 tablespoon sesame seeds

- Salt and pepper to taste

- Chopped green onions, for garnish

Instructions:

1.   Preheat your Instant Vortex Plus Dual Air Fryer to 200°C using the Air Fry function.

2.   In a bowl, mix together soy sauce, honey, sesame oil, grated ginger, minced garlic, sesame seeds, salt, and pepper.

3.   Brush each mahi mahi fillet with the sesame ginger glaze, coating both sides.

4.   Place the glazed mahi mahi fillets in the air fryer basket and cook for 8-10 minutes until fish is cooked through and flakes easily with a fork.

5.   Serve hot, garnished with chopped green onions.

Nutritional Info: Calories: 220 | Fat: 8g | Carbs: 8g | Protein: 30g

Prep: 20 mins | Cook: 12 mins | Serves: 4

Ingredients:

- 4 whole trout, cleaned and gutted
- 100g crumbled feta cheese
- 50g chopped black olives
- 2 tablespoons chopped fresh parsley
- 1 lemon, sliced
- Salt and pepper to taste
- Olive oil, for drizzling

Instructions:

1. Preheat your Instant Vortex Plus Dual Air Fryer to 180°C using the Air Fry function.

2. In a bowl, mix together crumbled feta cheese, chopped black olives, chopped fresh parsley, salt, and pepper.

3. Stuff each trout with the feta and olive mixture, then place lemon slices on top.

4. Drizzle olive oil over the stuffed trout.

5. Place the stuffed trout in the air fryer basket and cook for 10-12 minutes until fish is cooked through and flakes easily with a fork.

6. Serve hot, garnished with extra chopped parsley if desired.

Nutritional Info: Calories: 280 | Fat: 12g | Carbs: 3g | Protein: 38g

SPICY TUNA POKE BOWLS WITH AVOCADO

Prep: 20 mins | Cook: 0 mins | Serves: 4

Ingredients:

- 400g sushi-grade tuna, cubed
- 2 tablespoons soy sauce
- 1 tablespoon sesame oil
- 1 tablespoon rice vinegar
- 1 teaspoon Sriracha sauce
- 1 avocado, sliced
- 2 cups cooked sushi rice
- 1/2 cucumber, thinly sliced
- 1/4 cup sliced radishes
- 2 tablespoons chopped green onions
- 1 tablespoon sesame seeds
- Nori strips, for garnish

Instructions:

1. In a bowl, mix together cubed tuna, soy sauce, sesame oil, rice vinegar, and Sriracha sauce.

2. Divide cooked sushi rice among serving bowls.

3. Top each bowl with marinated tuna, sliced avocado, cucumber slices, sliced radishes, chopped green onions, sesame seeds, and nori strips.

4. Serve immediately and enjoy!

Nutritional Info: Calories: 350 | Fat: 15g | Carbs: 28g | Protein: 26g

Prep: 20 mins | Cook: 8 mins | Serves: 4

Ingredients:

- 500g white fish fillets (such as cod or tilapia)

- 8 small flour tortillas

- 1 cup shredded purple cabbage

- 1/2 cup shredded carrots

- 1/4 cup chopped fresh cilantro

- 1/4 cup mayonnaise

- 1 tablespoon lime juice

- 1 teaspoon chili powder

- 1/2 teaspoon cumin

- Salt and pepper to taste

- Lime wedges, for serving

Instructions:

1. Preheat your Instant Vortex Plus Dual Air Fryer to 200°C using the Air Fry function.

2. Season fish fillets with chili powder, cumin, salt, and pepper.

3. Place fish fillets in the air fryer basket and cook for 6-8 minutes until fish is cooked through and flakes easily with a fork.

4. Meanwhile, prepare the cabbage slaw by mixing together shredded purple cabbage, shredded carrots, chopped cilantro, mayonnaise, lime juice, salt, and pepper in a bowl.

5. Warm tortillas in the air fryer for 1-2 minutes.

6. Assemble tacos by filling each tortilla with cooked fish and cabbage slaw.

7. Serve hot, garnished with lime wedges.

Nutritional Info: Calories: 320 | Fat: 12g | Carbs: 30g | Protein: 24g

Prep: 10 mins | Cook: 10 mins | Serves: 4

Ingredients:

- 4 salmon fillets, about 150g each
- 2 tablespoons honey
- 2 tablespoons soy sauce
- 1 tablespoon rice vinegar
- 2 cloves garlic, minced
- 1 teaspoon grated ginger
- Sesame seeds, for garnish
- Chopped green onions, for garnish

Instructions:

1. Preheat your Instant Vortex Plus Dual Air Fryer to 200°C using the Air Fry function.

2. In a small saucepan, combine honey, soy sauce, rice vinegar, minced garlic, and grated ginger. Cook over medium heat until slightly thickened.

3. Brush salmon fillets with the honey garlic glaze, reserving some for serving.

4. Place the glazed salmon fillets in the air fryer basket and cook for 8-10 minutes until fish is cooked through.

5. Serve hot, garnished with sesame seeds, chopped green onions, and extra honey garlic glaze.

Nutritional Info: Calories: 280 | Fat: 12g | Carbs: 14g | Protein: 26g

HERB-ROASTED WHOLE CHICKEN

Prep: 15 mins | Cook: 1 hour 30 mins | Serves: 4

Ingredients:

- 1 whole chicken (about 1.5 kg)
- 2 tablespoons olive oil
- 2 teaspoons dried rosemary
- 2 teaspoons dried thyme
- 2 teaspoons dried oregano
- Salt and pepper to taste

Instructions:

1. Preheat your Instant Vortex Plus Dual Air Fryer to 180°C using the "Roast" function.

2. In a small bowl, mix together olive oil, rosemary, thyme, oregano, salt, and pepper to make a herb rub.

3. Pat the chicken dry with paper towels, then rub the herb mixture all over the chicken, including under the skin.

4. Place the seasoned chicken in the air fryer basket breast side down and cook for 45 minutes.

5. After 45 minutes, flip the chicken breast side up and continue cooking for another 45 minutes or until the internal temperature reaches 75°C.

6. Once cooked, remove the chicken from the air fryer, let it rest for 10 minutes before carving.

Nutritional Info (per serving): Calories: 320 | Fat: 18g | Carbs: 0g | Protein: 40g

Prep: 15 mins | Cook: 15 mins | Serves: 4

Ingredients:

- 500g chicken breast fillets, cut into strips
- 1 cup breadcrumbs
- 1 teaspoon paprika
- 1 teaspoon garlic powder
- Salt and pepper to taste
- 2 eggs, beaten

Instructions:

1. Preheat your Instant Vortex Plus Dual Air Fryer to 200°C using the "Air Fry" function.

2. In a shallow bowl, mix breadcrumbs, paprika, garlic powder, salt, and pepper.

3. Dip each chicken strip into the beaten eggs, then coat with the breadcrumb mixture.

4. Place the coated chicken strips in a single layer in the air fryer basket.

5. Air fry the chicken tenders for 12-15 minutes or until golden brown and crispy, flipping halfway through.

6. While the chicken is cooking, prepare your favorite dipping sauce.

Nutritional Info (per serving): Calories: 280 | Fat: 8g | Carbs: 18g | Protein: 30g

Prep: 10 mins | Cook: 25 mins | Serves: 4

Ingredients:

- 8 chicken thighs, bone-in and skin-on

- 4 tablespoons honey

- 3 tablespoons wholegrain mustard

- 2 cloves garlic, minced

- Salt and pepper to taste

Instructions:

1. Preheat your Instant Vortex Plus Dual Air Fryer to 180°C using the "Air Fry" function.

2. In a small bowl, mix together honey, mustard, minced garlic, salt, and pepper to make the marinade.

3. Place the chicken thighs in a large bowl and pour the marinade over them, ensuring they are well coated.

4. Arrange the chicken thighs in a single layer in the air fryer basket, skin side up.

5. Air fry the chicken thighs for 20-25 minutes or until they reach an internal temperature of 75°C.

6. Serve the honey mustard chicken thighs hot, garnished with fresh herbs if desired.

Nutritional Info (per serving): Calories: 380 | Fat: 20g | Carbs: 15g | Protein: 35g

Prep: 10 mins | Cook: 25 mins | Serves: 4

Ingredients:

- 1 kg chicken wings

- 1 cup BBQ sauce

- Salt and pepper to taste

- Ranch dressing for dipping

Instructions:

1. Preheat your Instant Vortex Plus Dual Air Fryer to 200°C using the "Air Fry" function.

2. Season the chicken wings with salt and pepper, then place them in a large bowl.

3. Pour BBQ sauce over the chicken wings and toss until evenly coated.

4. Arrange the chicken wings in a single layer in the air fryer basket.

5. Air fry the chicken wings for 20-25 minutes, flipping halfway through, until they are crispy and cooked through.

6. Serve the BBQ chicken wings hot with ranch dressing for dipping.

Nutritional Info (per serving): Calories: 420 | Fat: 22g | Carbs: 25g | Protein: 30g

Prep: 10 mins | Cook: 30 mins | Serves: 4

Ingredients:

- 8 chicken drumsticks
- 2 tablespoons olive oil
- 3 cloves garlic, minced
- Zest and juice of 1 lemon
- 1 teaspoon dried oregano
- Salt and pepper to taste

Instructions:

1. Preheat your Instant Vortex Plus Dual Air Fryer to 200°C using the "Roast" function.

2. In a small bowl, mix together olive oil, minced garlic, lemon zest, lemon juice, dried oregano, salt, and pepper.

3. Pat the chicken drumsticks dry with paper towels, then rub the lemon garlic mixture all over them.

4. Place the seasoned chicken drumsticks in the air fryer basket in a single layer.

5. Air fry the chicken drumsticks for 25-30 minutes or until golden brown and cooked through, turning halfway through.

6. Serve the lemon garlic roast chicken drumsticks hot, garnished with fresh herbs if desired.

Nutritional Info (per serving): Calories: 280 | Fat: 12g | Carbs: 2g | Protein: 38g

Prep: 15 mins | Cook: 20 mins | Serves: 4

Ingredients:

- 500g ground turkey

- 1/4 cup breadcrumbs

- 1/4 cup grated Parmesan cheese

- 1 egg, lightly beaten

- 2 cloves garlic, minced

- 1 teaspoon dried oregano

- 1 teaspoon dried basil

- Salt and pepper to taste

- 2 cups marinara sauce

Instructions:

1. Preheat your Instant Vortex Plus Dual Air Fryer to 180°C using the "Air Fry" function.

2. In a large bowl, mix together ground turkey, breadcrumbs, Parmesan cheese, egg, minced garlic, dried oregano, dried basil, salt, and pepper until well combined.

3. Shape the mixture into meatballs about 1 inch in diameter.

4. Place the turkey meatballs in a single layer in the air fryer basket.

5. Air fry the meatballs for 15-20 minutes or until cooked through, shaking the basket halfway through.

6. Serve the turkey meatballs hot with marinara sauce, garnished with fresh herbs if desired.

Nutritional Info (per serving): Calories: 280 | Fat: 12g | Carbs: 9g | Protein: 32g

Prep: 10 mins | Cook: 25 mins | Serves: 4

Ingredients:

- 1 kg chicken wings

- 1/4 cup grated Parmesan cheese

- 2 cloves garlic, minced

- 2 tablespoons melted butter

- Salt and pepper to taste

- Chopped parsley for garnish

Instructions:

1. Preheat your Instant Vortex Plus Dual Air Fryer to 200°C using the "Air Fry" function.

2. In a bowl, mix together grated Parmesan cheese, minced garlic, melted butter, salt, and pepper.

3. Toss the chicken wings in the garlic Parmesan mixture until evenly coated.

4. Place the coated chicken wings in a single layer in the air fryer basket.

5. Air fry the chicken wings for 20-25 minutes, flipping halfway through, until crispy and golden brown.

6. Once cooked, sprinkle with chopped parsley before serving.

Nutritional Info (per serving): Calories: 420 | Fat: 28g | Carbs: 2g | Protein: 38g

Prep: 15 mins | Cook: 10 mins | Serves: 4

Ingredients:

- 2 cups cooked shredded chicken

- 1/2 cup BBQ sauce

- 4 large flour tortillas

- 1 cup shredded Pepper Jack cheese

- 1/2 cup diced red onion

- 1/4 cup chopped fresh cilantro

- Olive oil or cooking spray

Instructions:

1. In a bowl, mix shredded chicken with BBQ sauce until well coated.

2. Lay out a tortilla on a flat surface, then spread an even layer of BBQ chicken over half of the tortilla.

3. Sprinkle shredded Pepper Jack cheese, diced red onion, and chopped cilantro over the chicken.

4. Fold the other half of the tortilla over the filling to create a half-moon shape.

5. Preheat your Instant Vortex Plus Dual Air Fryer to 180°C using the "Air Fry" function.

6. Lightly brush or spray both sides of the quesadilla with olive oil or cooking spray.

7. Place the quesadilla in the air fryer basket and air fry for 5 minutes on each side until golden and crispy.

8. Repeat with the remaining tortillas and filling.

9. Once cooked, slice the quesadillas into wedges and serve hot with extra BBQ sauce for dipping.

Nutritional Info (per serving): Calories: 420 | Fat: 18g | Carbs: 36g | Protein: 28g

Prep: 10 mins | Cook: 20 mins | Serves: 4

Ingredients:

- 4 chicken breast fillets

- 2 tablespoons olive oil

- Zest and juice of 1 lemon

- 2 cloves garlic, minced

- 1 tablespoon chopped fresh rosemary

- Salt and pepper to taste

Instructions:

1. In a bowl, mix together olive oil, lemon zest, lemon juice, minced garlic, chopped rosemary, salt, and pepper.

2. Place the chicken breast fillets in a shallow dish and pour the marinade over them, turning to coat evenly. Let them marinate for at least 10 minutes.

3. Preheat your Instant Vortex Plus Dual Air Fryer to 200°C using the "Roast" function.

4. Place the marinated chicken breast fillets in the air fryer basket in a single layer.

5. Air fry the chicken breast fillets for 18-20 minutes, flipping halfway through, until cooked through and golden brown.

6. Serve the rosemary lemon chicken breast hot, garnished with extra chopped rosemary and lemon slices if desired.

Nutritional Info (per serving): Calories: 280 | Fat: 12g | Carbs: 2g | Protein: 38g

Prep: 10 mins | Cook: 25 mins | Serves: 4

Ingredients:

- 8 chicken drumsticks

- 2 tablespoons olive oil

- 2 tablespoons BBQ seasoning rub

- Salt and pepper to taste

Instructions:

1. Pat the chicken drumsticks dry with paper towels, then rub them all over with olive oil.

2. Season the chicken drumsticks generously with BBQ seasoning rub, salt, and pepper.

3. Preheat your Instant Vortex Plus Dual Air Fryer to 200°C using the "Air Fry" function.

4. Place the seasoned chicken drumsticks in the air fryer basket in a single layer.

5. Air fry the chicken drumsticks for 20-25 minutes, flipping halfway through, until crispy and cooked through.

6. Serve the crispy chicken drumsticks hot, garnished with fresh herbs if desired.

Nutritional Info (per serving): Calories: 320 | Fat: 18g | Carbs: 0g | Protein: 40g

Prep: 10 mins | Cook: 25 mins | Serves: 4

Ingredients:

- 8 chicken thighs, bone-in and skin-on

- 1/2 cup orange marmalade

- 2 tablespoons soy sauce

- 2 cloves garlic, minced

- 1 teaspoon grated ginger

- Salt and pepper to taste

- Sesame seeds and sliced green onions for garnish

Instructions:

1. Preheat your Instant Vortex Plus Dual Air Fryer to 200°C using the "Roast" function.

2. In a small saucepan, combine orange marmalade, soy sauce, minced garlic, grated ginger, salt, and pepper. Heat over low heat until the marmalade is melted and the sauce is well combined.

3. Pat the chicken thighs dry with paper towels, then brush them generously with the orange glaze.

4. Place the glazed chicken thighs in the air fryer basket in a single layer.

5. Air fry the chicken thighs for 20-25 minutes or until cooked through, brushing with more glaze halfway through.

6. Once cooked, sprinkle with sesame seeds and sliced green onions before serving.

Nutritional Info (per serving): Calories: 380 | Fat: 20g | Carbs: 20g | Protein: 30g

Prep: 15 mins | Cook: 20 mins | Serves: 4

Ingredients:

- 4 boneless, skinless chicken breasts
- 1 cup breadcrumbs
- 1/2 cup grated Parmesan cheese
- 1 teaspoon dried basil
- 1 teaspoon dried oregano
- 1 teaspoon garlic powder
- Salt and pepper to taste
- 1 cup marinara sauce
- 1 cup shredded mozzarella cheese
- Fresh basil leaves for garnish

Instructions:

1. Preheat your Air Fryer to 200°C using the "Air Fry" function.

2. In a shallow bowl, mix together breadcrumbs, Parmesan cheese, dried basil, dried oregano, garlic powder, salt, and pepper.

3. Coat each chicken breast with the breadcrumb mixture, pressing to adhere.

4. Place the coated chicken breasts in the air fryer basket in a single layer.

5. Air fry the chicken breasts for 15 minutes, then top each breast with marinara sauce and shredded mozzarella cheese.

6. Continue air frying for another 5 minutes or until the cheese is melted and bubbly.

7. Once cooked, garnish with fresh basil leaves before serving.

Nutritional Info (per serving): Calories: 320 | Fat: 12g | Carbs: 15g | Protein: 40g

Prep: 20 mins | Cook: 15 mins | Serves: 4

Ingredients:

- 4 boneless, skinless chicken breasts

- 1 cup plain flour

- 2 eggs, beaten and 1 teaspoon paprika

- 1 cup breadcrumbs

- 1 teaspoon garlic powder

- Salt and pepper to taste

- 4 burger buns and Coleslaw, for serving

- Mayonnaise or your favorite sauce, for serving

Instructions:

1.   Preheat your Air Fryer to 200°C using the "Air Fry" function.

2.   Set up a breading station with three shallow bowls: one with flour, one with beaten eggs, and one with breadcrumbs mixed with paprika, garlic powder, salt, and pepper.

3.   Dredge each chicken breast in flour, then dip into the beaten eggs, and finally coat with the breadcrumb mixture, pressing gently to adhere.

4.   Place the breaded chicken breasts in the air fryer basket in a single layer.

5.   Air fry the chicken breasts for 12-15 minutes or until golden brown and cooked through.

6.   Toast the burger buns in the air fryer for 1-2 minutes.

7.   Assemble the sandwiches by placing a crispy chicken breast on each bun, topping with coleslaw, and drizzling with mayonnaise or your favorite sauce.

   8. Serve the crispy chicken sandwiches immediately.

Nutritional Info (per serving): Calories: 420 | Fat: 12g | Carbs: 45g | Protein: 35g

JUICY AIR FRYER BURGERS WITH CHEESE

Prep: 15 mins | Cook: 15 mins | Serves: 4

Ingredients:

- 500g lean beef mince
- 1 onion, finely chopped
- 1 egg
- 1 tbsp Worcestershire sauce
- Salt and pepper to taste
- 4 slices cheddar cheese
- Burger buns and toppings of your choice

Instructions:

1. In a bowl, mix together the beef mince, chopped onion, egg, Worcestershire sauce, salt, and pepper until well combined.

2. Shape the mixture into 4 burger patties.

3. Preheat your Instant Vortex Plus Dual Air Fryer to 180°C using the Air Fry function.

4. Place the burger patties in the air fryer basket and cook for 10-12 minutes, flipping halfway through, until cooked through.

5. In the last 2 minutes of cooking, place a slice of cheese on each burger and continue cooking until the cheese is melted.

6. Serve the burgers on buns with your favorite toppings.

Nutritional Info (per serving): Calories: 350 | Fat: 18g | Carbs: 25g | Protein: 25g

Prep: 20 mins | Cook: 15 mins | Serves: 4

Ingredients:

- 500g beef sirloin, cut into cubes

- 1 red bell pepper, cut into chunks

- 1 green bell pepper, cut into chunks

- 1 red onion, cut into chunks

- 8 cherry tomatoes

- 8 button mushrooms

- 2 tbsp olive oil

- Salt and pepper to taste

- Wooden skewers, soaked in water

Instructions:

1. Thread the beef cubes and vegetables onto the soaked wooden skewers, alternating between the ingredients.

2. Brush the kabobs with olive oil and season with salt and pepper.

3. Preheat your Instant Vortex Plus Dual Air Fryer to 200°C using the Air Fry function.

4. Place the kabobs in the air fryer basket and cook for 12-15 minutes, turning halfway through, until the beef is cooked to your desired doneness and the vegetables are tender.

5. Serve the beef kabobs hot with your favorite dipping sauce or side dishes.

Nutritional Info (per serving): Calories: 280 | Fat: 15g | Carbs: 8g | Protein: 30g

Prep: 10 mins | Cook: 20 mins | Serves: 2

Ingredients:

- 2 pork chops

- 1 tbsp olive oil

- Salt and pepper to taste

- 2 apples, peeled and sliced

- 1 tbsp butter

- 1 tbsp brown sugar

- 1/2 tsp cinnamon

Instructions:

1. Season the pork chops with salt and pepper.

2. Preheat your Instant Vortex Plus Dual Air Fryer to 200°C using the Air Fry function.

3. Place the pork chops in the air fryer basket and cook for 18-20 minutes, flipping halfway through, until golden brown and cooked through.

4. While the pork chops are cooking, prepare the apple compote. In a saucepan, melt the butter over medium heat.

5. Add the sliced apples, brown sugar, and cinnamon to the saucepan. Cook, stirring occasionally, until the apples are soft and caramelized.

6. Serve the crispy pork chops with the apple compote on top.

Nutritional Info (per serving): Calories: 320 | Fat: 15g | Carbs: 20g | Protein: 25g

Prep: 15 mins | Cook: 20 mins | Serves: 4

Ingredients:

- 4 Italian sausages

- 2 bell peppers (any color), sliced

- 1 onion, sliced

- 2 cloves garlic, minced

- 2 tbsp olive oil

- Salt and pepper to taste

- Italian seasoning to taste

Instructions:

1. Preheat your Instant Vortex Plus Dual Air Fryer to 180°C using the Air Fry function.

2. In a bowl, toss the sliced bell peppers, onion, minced garlic, olive oil, salt, pepper, and Italian seasoning until well coated.

3. Place the seasoned vegetables in the air fryer basket.

4. Add the Italian sausages to the air fryer basket alongside the vegetables.

5. Cook for 18-20 minutes, shaking the basket halfway through, until the sausages are cooked through and the vegetables are tender.

6. Serve the Italian sausages and peppers hot, optionally with crusty bread or over pasta.

Nutritional Info (per serving): Calories: 380 | Fat: 25g | Carbs: 10g | Protein: 25g

Prep: 15 mins | Cook: 40 mins | Serves: 2

Ingredients:

- 500g baby back ribs

- Salt and pepper to taste

- 200ml BBQ sauce

- 2 tbsp brown sugar

- 1 tbsp Worcestershire sauce

- 1 tbsp apple cider vinegar

Instructions:

1. Season the baby back ribs with salt and pepper.

2. Preheat your Instant Vortex Plus Dual Air Fryer to 180°C using the Air Fry function.

3. Place the seasoned ribs in the air fryer basket and cook for 30 minutes.

4. While the ribs are cooking, prepare the BBQ sauce. In a saucepan, combine the BBQ sauce, brown sugar, Worcestershire sauce, and apple cider vinegar. Heat over medium heat until the sugar is dissolved and the sauce is heated through.

5. Brush the cooked ribs with the homemade BBQ sauce.

6. Increase the temperature to 200°C and cook for an additional 10 minutes, brushing with more BBQ sauce halfway through.

7. Serve the BBQ baby back ribs hot with extra sauce on the side.

Nutritional Info (per serving): Calories: 450 | Fat: 25g | Carbs: 25g | Protein: 30g

Prep: 5 mins | Cook: 15 mins | Serves: 2

Ingredients:

- 2 ham steaks

- 2 tbsp honey

- 1 tbsp Dijon mustard

- 1 tbsp olive oil

- Salt and pepper to taste

Instructions:

1. Preheat your Instant Vortex Plus Dual Air Fryer to 180°C using the Air Fry function.

2. In a small bowl, mix together the honey, Dijon mustard, olive oil, salt, and pepper.

3. Brush the honey glaze over both sides of the ham steaks.

4. Place the glazed ham steaks in the air fryer basket.

5. Cook for 12-15 minutes, flipping halfway through, until heated through and caramelized.

6. Serve the honey glazed ham steaks hot with your favorite sides.

Nutritional Info (per serving): Calories: 280 | Fat: 12g | Carbs: 15g | Protein: 30g

Prep: 10 mins | Cook: 25 mins | Serves: 2

Ingredients:

- 500g beef short ribs

- 3 tbsp soy sauce

- 2 tbsp brown sugar

- 1 tbsp sesame oil

- 2 cloves garlic, minced

- 1 tsp ginger, grated

- 1 tsp gochujang (Korean chili paste)

- 1 green onion, chopped (for garnish)

Instructions:

1. In a bowl, mix together the soy sauce, brown sugar, sesame oil, minced garlic, grated ginger, and gochujang.

2. Marinate the beef short ribs in the sauce for at least 30 minutes.

3. Preheat your Instant Vortex Plus Dual Air Fryer to 200°C using the Air Fry function.

4. Place the marinated short ribs in the air fryer basket.

5. Cook for 20-25 minutes, flipping halfway through, until caramelized and cooked to your desired doneness.

6. Garnish with chopped green onions before serving.

Nutritional Info (per serving): Calories: 380 | Fat: 20g | Carbs: 15g | Protein: 35g

Prep: 10 mins | Cook: 15 mins | Serves: 2

Ingredients:

- 4 lamb chops
- 2 tbsp olive oil
- Salt and pepper to taste
- 2 tbsp fresh mint leaves, chopped
- 1 tbsp lemon juice
- 1 tsp honey

Instructions:

1. Preheat your Instant Vortex Plus Dual Air Fryer to 200°C using the Air Fry function.

2. Rub the lamb chops with olive oil and season with salt and pepper.

3. Place the seasoned lamb chops in the air fryer basket.

4. Cook for 12-15 minutes, flipping halfway through, until golden brown and crispy.

5. While the lamb chops are cooking, prepare the mint sauce. In a small bowl, combine the chopped mint leaves, lemon juice, and honey.

6. Serve the crispy lamb chops hot with the mint sauce drizzled over the top.

Nutritional Info (per serving): Calories: 350 | Fat: 22g | Carbs: 2g | Protein: 35g

GARLIC BUTTER STEAK BITES

Prep: 10 mins | Cook: 10 mins | Serves: 4

Ingredients:

- 500g beef steak, cut into bite-sized pieces

- 4 tbsp butter, melted

- 4 cloves garlic, minced

- 1 tbsp Worcestershire sauce

- Salt and pepper to taste

- Chopped fresh parsley for garnish

Instructions:

1. Preheat your Instant Vortex Plus Dual Air Fryer to 200°C using the Air Fry function.

2. In a bowl, combine the melted butter, minced garlic, Worcestershire sauce, salt, and pepper.

3. Add the steak pieces to the bowl and toss until evenly coated.

4. Place the steak bites in the air fryer basket in a single layer.

5. Cook for 8-10 minutes, shaking the basket halfway through, until the steak is cooked to your desired doneness.

6. Garnish with chopped fresh parsley before serving.

Nutritional Info (per serving): Calories: 280 | Fat: 20g | Carbs: 2g | Protein: 25g

Prep: 15 mins | Cook: 15 mins | Serves: 4

Ingredients:

- 500g ground lamb
- 1 onion, grated
- 2 cloves garlic, minced
- 2 tbsp fresh parsley, chopped
- 1 tsp ground cumin
- 1 tsp ground coriander
- 1/2 tsp ground cinnamon
- Salt and pepper to taste
- 4 tbsp Greek yogurt, for serving
- Chopped fresh mint for garnish

Instructions:

1. In a bowl, mix together the ground lamb, grated onion, minced garlic, chopped parsley, ground cumin, ground coriander, ground cinnamon, salt, and pepper until well combined.

2. Divide the mixture into equal portions and shape each portion into a sausage-shaped kofta.

3. Preheat your Instant Vortex Plus Dual Air Fryer to 180°C using the Air Fry function.

4. Place the lamb koftas in the air fryer basket.

5. Cook for 12-15 minutes, turning halfway through, until browned and cooked through.

6. Serve the Moroccan spiced lamb koftas hot with Greek yogurt and chopped fresh mint.

Nutritional Info (per serving): Calories: 320 | Fat: 25g | Carbs: 4g | Protein: 20g

Prep: 15 mins | Cook: 25 mins | Serves: 4

Ingredients:

- 8 chicken drumsticks
- 1 cup buttermilk
- 1 cup breadcrumbs
- 2 tbsp Cajun seasoning
- 1 tsp garlic powder
- 1 tsp onion powder
- Salt and pepper to taste
- Cooking spray

Instructions:

1. Place the chicken drumsticks in a bowl and cover them with buttermilk. Let them marinate for at least 30 minutes.

2. In another bowl, mix together the breadcrumbs, Cajun seasoning, garlic powder, onion powder, salt, and pepper.

3. Preheat your Instant Vortex Plus Dual Air Fryer to 200°C using the Air Fry function.

4. Remove the drumsticks from the buttermilk and coat them evenly in the breadcrumb mixture.

5. Spray the air fryer basket with cooking spray.

6. Place the coated drumsticks in the air fryer basket in a single layer.

7. Cook for 20-25 minutes, turning halfway through, until the chicken is golden brown and cooked through.

8. Serve the Cajun fried chicken drumsticks hot with your favorite dipping sauce.

Nutritional Info (per serving): Calories: 280 | Fat: 12g | Carbs: 10g | Protein: 30g

Prep: 10 mins | Cook: 30 mins | Serves: 4

Ingredients:

- 500g beef roast

- 4 cloves garlic, minced

- 2 tbsp fresh rosemary, chopped

- 2 tbsp olive oil

- Salt and pepper to taste

Instructions:

1. Preheat your Instant Vortex Plus Dual Air Fryer to 200°C using the Air Fry function.

2. In a small bowl, mix together the minced garlic, chopped rosemary, olive oil, salt, and pepper.

3. Rub the garlic and rosemary mixture all over the beef roast.

4. Place the seasoned roast in the air fryer basket.

5. Cook for 25-30 minutes, depending on the desired level of doneness.

6. Let the roast rest for 10 minutes before slicing.

7. Serve the rosemary garlic roast beef hot with your favorite side dishes.

Nutritional Info (per serving): Calories: 350 | Fat: 18g | Carbs: 0g | Protein: 45g

Prep: 10 mins | Cook: 25 mins | Serves: 4

Ingredients:

- 500g pork tenderloin

- 8 slices bacon

- 2 tbsp maple syrup

- 1 tbsp Dijon mustard

- Salt and pepper to taste

Instructions:

1. Preheat your Instant Vortex Plus Dual Air Fryer to 200°C using the Air Fry function.

2. Season the pork tenderloin with salt and pepper.

3. In a small bowl, mix together the maple syrup and Dijon mustard.

4. Wrap each slice of bacon around the pork tenderloin and secure with toothpicks.

5. Brush the maple-Dijon mixture over the bacon-wrapped pork tenderloin.

6. Place the pork tenderloin in the air fryer basket.

7. Cook for 20-25 minutes, until the bacon is crispy and the pork is cooked through.

8. Let the pork tenderloin rest for 5 minutes before slicing.

9. Serve the maple glazed bacon-wrapped pork tenderloin hot with roasted vegetables or mashed potatoes.

Nutritional Info (per serving): Calories: 320 | Fat: 18g | Carbs: 8g | Protein: 35g

Prep: 15 mins | Cook: 20 mins | Serves: 4

Ingredients:

- 8 chicken thighs, bone-in, skin-on
- 2 tbsp jerk seasoning
- 2 tbsp olive oil
- Juice of 1 lime
- Salt to taste
- Chopped fresh cilantro for garnish

Instructions:

1. Preheat your Instant Vortex Plus Dual Air Fryer to 200°C using the Air Fry function.

2. In a bowl, toss the chicken thighs with jerk seasoning, olive oil, lime juice, and salt until evenly coated.

3. Place the seasoned chicken thighs in the air fryer basket.

4. Cook for 18-20 minutes, flipping halfway through, until the chicken is golden brown and cooked through.

5. Garnish with chopped fresh cilantro before serving.

Nutritional Info (per serving): Calories: 340 | Fat: 22g | Carbs: 2g | Protein: 30g

PARMESAN ZUCCHINI FRIES

Prep: 15 mins | Cook: 12 mins | Serves: 4

Ingredients:

- 2 large zucchinis, cut into fries
- 1 cup breadcrumbs
- 1/2 cup grated Parmesan cheese
- 1 tsp garlic powder
- Salt and pepper to taste
- 2 eggs, beaten

Instructions:

1. Preheat your Instant Vortex Plus Dual Air Fryer to 200°C using the "Air Fry" function.

2. In a shallow dish, mix breadcrumbs, Parmesan cheese, garlic powder, salt, and pepper.

3. Dip zucchini fries into beaten eggs, then coat them in the breadcrumb mixture.

4. Place the coated zucchini fries in the air fryer basket in a single layer.

5. Cook for 12 minutes, flipping halfway through, until the fries are golden and crispy.

6. Serve hot with your favorite dipping sauce.

Nutritional Info: Calories: 180 | Fat: 8g | Carbs: 20g | Protein: 8g

CRISPY ASPARAGUS SPEARS WITH LEMON GARLIC AIOLI

Prep: 10 mins | Cook: 8 mins | Serves: 4

Ingredients:

- 1 bunch asparagus spears, trimmed
- 1/2 cup breadcrumbs
- 1/4 cup grated Parmesan cheese
- 1 tsp garlic powder
- Salt and pepper to taste
- Cooking spray

Instructions:

1. Preheat your Instant Vortex Plus Dual Air Fryer to 200°C using the "Air Fry" function.

2. In a shallow dish, mix breadcrumbs, Parmesan cheese, garlic powder, salt, and pepper.

3. Dip asparagus spears into water, then coat them in the breadcrumb mixture.

4. Place the coated asparagus spears in the air fryer basket and spray with cooking spray.

5. Cook for 8 minutes until the asparagus is tender and crispy.

6. Meanwhile, prepare the lemon garlic aioli by mixing mayonnaise, lemon juice, minced garlic, and a pinch of salt.

7. Serve the crispy asparagus spears with the lemon garlic aioli for dipping.

Nutritional Info: Calories: 120 | Fat: 5g | Carbs: 15g | Protein: 6g

Prep: 10 mins | Cook: 20 mins | Serves: 4

Ingredients:

- 500g baby potatoes, halved
- 2 tbsp olive oil
- 2 cloves garlic, minced
- 1 tsp dried thyme
- 1 tsp dried rosemary
- Salt and pepper to taste
- Fresh parsley for garnish

Instructions:

1. Preheat your Instant Vortex Plus Dual Air Fryer to 200°C using the "Roast" function.

2. In a bowl, toss the halved baby potatoes with olive oil, minced garlic, dried thyme, dried rosemary, salt, and pepper until evenly coated.

3. Place the seasoned potatoes in the air fryer basket in a single layer.

4. Roast for 20 minutes, shaking the basket halfway through, until the potatoes are golden brown and crispy on the outside and tender on the inside.

5. Garnish with fresh parsley before serving.

6. Enjoy these garlic herb roasted potatoes as a flavorful side dish to any meal!

Nutritional Info: Calories: 180 | Fat: 7g | Carbs: 25g | Protein: 3g

Prep: 15 mins | Cook: 15 mins | Serves: 4

Ingredients:

- 1 small butternut squash, peeled and cut into fries

- 2 tbsp olive oil

- 1 tbsp maple syrup

- 1 tbsp Dijon mustard

- Salt and pepper to taste

For Maple Dijon Dip:

1/4 cup Greek yogurt

1 tbsp maple syrup

1 tsp Dijon mustard

Salt and pepper to taste

Instructions:

1.   Preheat your Air Fryer to 200°C using the "Air Fry" function.

2.   In a bowl, toss the butternut squash fries with olive oil, maple syrup, salt, and pepper until evenly coated.

3.   Place the seasoned butternut squash fries in the air fryer basket in a single layer.

4.   Air fry for 15 minutes, shaking the basket halfway through, until the fries are golden and crispy.

5.   Meanwhile, prepare the maple Dijon dip by combining Greek yogurt, maple syrup, Dijon mustard, salt, and pepper in a small bowl.

6.   Serve the butternut squash fries hot with the maple Dijon dip on the side.

7.   Enjoy this healthier alternative to traditional fries!

Nutritional Info: Calories: 150 | Fat: 5g | Carbs: 25g | Protein: 3g

Prep: 10 mins | Cook: 20 mins | Serves: 4

Ingredients:

- 500g carrots, peeled and sliced into sticks

- 2 tbsp olive oil

- 2 tbsp balsamic vinegar

- 1 tbsp honey

- Salt and pepper to taste

- Fresh parsley for garnish

Instructions:

1. Preheat your Instant Vortex Plus Dual Air Fryer to 200°C using the "Roast" function.

2. In a bowl, toss the carrot sticks with olive oil, balsamic vinegar, honey, salt, and pepper until evenly coated.

3. Place the seasoned carrot sticks in the air fryer basket in a single layer.

4. Roast for 20 minutes, shaking the basket halfway through, until the carrots are tender and caramelized.

5. Garnish with fresh parsley before serving.

6. Enjoy these balsamic roasted carrots as a flavorful and nutritious side dish!

Nutritional Info: Calories: 120 | Fat: 7g | Carbs: 15g | Protein: 1g

Prep: 15 mins | Cook: 10 mins | Serves: 4

Ingredients:

- 300g green beans, trimmed
- 1 cup breadcrumbs
- 1/2 cup grated Parmesan cheese
- 1 tsp garlic powder
- Salt and pepper to taste
- Cooking spray
- 1/4 cup mayonnaise
- 1 tbsp Sriracha sauce

Instructions:

1. Preheat your Instant Vortex Plus Dual Air Fryer to 200°C using the "Air Fry" function.

2. In a shallow dish, mix breadcrumbs, Parmesan cheese, garlic powder, salt, and pepper.

3. Dip green beans into water, then coat them in the breadcrumb mixture.

4. Place the coated green beans in the air fryer basket and spray with cooking spray.

5. Air fry for 10 minutes until the green beans are crispy and golden brown.

6. Meanwhile, prepare the Sriracha mayo by combining mayonnaise and Sriracha sauce in a small bowl.

7. Serve the crispy green bean fries hot with the Sriracha mayo for dipping.

8. Enjoy this delicious and nutritious snack or side dish!

Nutritional Info: Calories: 150 | Fat: 8g | Carbs: 15g | Protein: 6g

Prep: 15 mins | Cook: 25 mins | Serves: 4

Ingredients:

- 4 large bell peppers, halved and seeds removed

- 1 cup cooked quinoa

- 1 cup black beans, drained and rinsed

- 1 cup corn kernels

- 1 cup grated cheddar cheese

- 1 tsp chili powder

- 1/2 tsp cumin

- Salt and pepper to taste

- Fresh cilantro for garnish

Instructions:

1. Preheat your Instant Vortex Plus Dual Air Fryer to 180°C using the "Bake" function.

2. In a bowl, mix cooked quinoa, black beans, corn kernels, grated cheddar cheese, chili powder, cumin, salt, and pepper.

3. Stuff each bell pepper half with the quinoa mixture, pressing down gently to compact.

4. Place the stuffed bell peppers in the air fryer basket.

5. Bake for 25 minutes until the peppers are tender and the filling is heated through.

6. Garnish with fresh cilantro before serving.

7. Enjoy these stuffed bell peppers as a wholesome and satisfying meal!

Nutritional Info: Calories: 300 | Fat: 10g | Carbs: 40g | Protein: 15g

Prep: 10 mins | Cook: 20 mins | Serves: 4

Ingredients:

- 2 large sweet potatoes, cut into wedges

- 2 tbsp olive oil

- 1 tbsp Cajun seasoning

- Salt and pepper to taste

Instructions:

1.   Preheat your Instant Vortex Plus Dual Air Fryer to 200°C using the "Air Fry" function.

2.   In a bowl, toss sweet potato wedges with olive oil, Cajun seasoning, salt, and pepper until evenly coated.

3.   Place the seasoned sweet potato wedges in the air fryer basket in a single layer.

4.   Air fry for 20 minutes until the sweet potatoes are crispy and golden brown.

5.   Serve hot as a tasty side dish or snack.

6.   Enjoy these Cajun-seasoned sweet potato wedges with your favorite dipping sauce!

Nutritional Info: Calories: 180 | Fat: 7g | Carbs: 25g | Protein: 2g

Prep: 10 mins | Cook: 15 mins | Serves: 4

Ingredients:

- 1 large eggplant, sliced into rounds

- 2 tbsp olive oil

- 1 tsp dried oregano

- 1 tsp dried basil

- 1/2 tsp garlic powder

- Salt and pepper to taste

- Lemon wedges for serving

Instructions:

1.   Preheat your Instant Vortex Plus Dual Air Fryer to 200°C using the "Roast" function.

2.   In a bowl, toss eggplant slices with olive oil, dried oregano, dried basil, garlic powder, salt, and pepper until evenly coated.

3.   Place the seasoned eggplant slices in the air fryer basket in a single layer.

4.   Roast for 15 minutes until the eggplant is tender and golden brown.

5.   Serve hot with a squeeze of fresh lemon juice.

6.   Enjoy these Mediterranean roasted eggplant slices as a flavorful side dish or appetizer!

Nutritional Info: Calories: 90 | Fat: 7g | Carbs: 8g | Protein: 1g

Prep: 10 mins | Cook: 12 mins | Serves: 4

Ingredients:

- 500g button mushrooms, cleaned and halved

- 2 tbsp unsalted butter

- 3 cloves garlic, minced

- 1 tsp dried thyme

- Salt and pepper to taste

- Fresh parsley for garnish

Instructions:

1. Preheat your Instant Vortex Plus Dual Air Fryer to 180°C using the "Air Fry" function.

2. In a microwave-safe bowl, melt the butter with minced garlic and dried thyme.

3. Toss the halved mushrooms in the garlic butter mixture until evenly coated.

4. Place the coated mushrooms in the air fryer basket.

5. Air fry for 12 minutes, shaking the basket halfway through, until the mushrooms are golden brown and tender.

6. Season with salt and pepper to taste.

7. Garnish with fresh parsley before serving.

8. Enjoy these garlic butter mushrooms as a flavorful side dish or topping for steak and pasta!

Nutritional Info: Calories: 80 | Fat: 6g | Carbs: 5g | Protein: 3g

Prep: 5 mins | Cook: 12 mins | Serves: 4

Ingredients:

- 4 ears of corn, husked
- 2 tbsp unsalted butter, melted
- 1 tsp chili powder
- Zest and juice of 1 lime
- Salt and pepper to taste
- Chopped cilantro for garnish

Instructions:

1. Preheat your Instant Vortex Plus Dual Air Fryer to 200°C using the "Air Fry" function.

2. In a small bowl, mix melted butter with chili powder, lime zest, lime juice, salt, and pepper.

3. Brush the seasoned butter mixture onto each ear of corn.

4. Place the corn on the cob in the air fryer basket.

5. Air fry for 12 minutes, turning halfway through, until the corn is tender and lightly charred.

6. Remove the corn from the air fryer and sprinkle with chopped cilantro before serving.

7. Enjoy this flavorful air fryer corn on the cob as a delicious summer side dish!

Nutritional Info: Calories: 120 | Fat: 6g | Carbs: 18g | Protein: 3g

CHAPTER 8: DESSERTS AND SWEETS

AIR FRYER APPLE HAND PIES

Prep: 20 mins | Cook: 15 mins | Makes: 6 hand pies

Ingredients:

- 2 sheets ready-rolled puff pastry

- 2 medium apples, peeled, cored, and diced

- 2 tablespoons granulated sugar

- 1 teaspoon ground cinnamon

- 1 tablespoon lemon juice

- 1 egg, beaten (for egg wash)

- Icing sugar, for dusting

Instructions:

1. Preheat your Instant Vortex Plus Dual Air Fryer to 180°C (350°F).

2. In a bowl, mix diced apples, granulated sugar, ground cinnamon, and lemon juice until well combined.

3. Cut each puff pastry sheet into 6 equal squares.

4. Place a spoonful of the apple mixture onto one half of each square.

5. Fold the pastry over the filling to create a triangle and press the edges firmly to seal.

6. Brush the tops of the hand pies with beaten egg for a golden finish.

7. Place the hand pies in the air fryer basket, leaving space between each pie.

8. Air fry at 180°C (350°F) for 12-15 minutes or until golden brown and crispy.

9. Once done, remove from the air fryer and let cool slightly.

10. Dust with icing sugar before serving.

Nutritional Info (per hand pie): Calories: 230 | Fat: 12g | Carbs: 28g | Protein: 3g

Prep: 15 mins | Cook: 10 mins | Serves: 4

Ingredients:

- 100g dark chocolate, chopped
- 50g unsalted butter
- 2 large eggs
- 50g caster sugar
- 30g plain flour and Pinch of salt
- Icing sugar, for dusting
- Fresh berries, to serve (optional)
- Vanilla ice cream, to serve (optional)

Instructions:

1. Preheat your Instant Vortex Plus Dual Air Fryer to 180°C (350°F).

2. In a heatproof bowl, melt the dark chocolate and butter together in the microwave or over a double boiler. Stir until smooth.

3. In a separate bowl, whisk together the eggs and caster sugar until light and fluffy.

4. Gradually pour the melted chocolate mixture into the egg mixture, whisking constantly.

5. Sift in the flour and salt, then gently fold until just combined.

6. Grease four ramekins with butter and dust with cocoa powder.

7. Divide the batter evenly among the ramekins.

8. Place the ramekins in the air fryer basket and air fry at 180°C (350°F) for 8-10 minutes, until the edges are set but the center is still gooey.

9. Carefully remove the ramekins from the air fryer and let them cool.

10. Dust with icing sugar and serve warm with fresh berries and vanilla ice cream, if desired.

Nutritional Info (per serving): Calories: 320 | Fat: 20g | Carbs: 30g | Protein: 5g

Prep: 15 mins | Cook: 8 mins | Makes: 24 donut holes

Ingredients:

- 250g plain flour and 2 teaspoons baking powder

- 1/2 teaspoon ground cinnamon

- 75g caster sugar and Pinch of salt

- 50g unsalted butter, melted and 1 large egg

- 1 teaspoon vanilla extract and 120ml milk

- 100g granulated sugar (for coating)

- 2 teaspoons ground cinnamon (for coating)

- 60g unsalted butter, melted (for dipping)

Instructions:

1. Preheat your Instant Vortex Plus Dual Air Fryer to 180°C (350°F).

2. In a large bowl, whisk together the flour, baking powder, ground cinnamon, salt, and caster sugar.

3. In another bowl, beat the egg, then stir in the milk, melted butter, and vanilla extract.

4. Pour the wet ingredients into the dry ingredients and mix.

5. Roll the dough into small balls, about 1-inch in diameter.

6. In a shallow bowl, mix together the granulated sugar and ground cinnamon for the coating.

7. Dip each dough ball into the melted butter, then roll in the cinnamon sugar mixture until coated.

8. Place the coated dough balls in a single layer in the air fryer basket, leaving space between each one.

9. Air fry at 180°C (350°F) for 6-8 minutes, until golden brown.

10. Once done, remove from the air fryer and let cool slightly.

Nutritional Info (per donut hole): Calories: 90 | Fat: 4g | Carbs: 12g | Protein: 1g

CHOCOLATE CHIP COOKIES

Prep: 15 mins | Cook: 10 mins | Makes: 18 cookies

Ingredients:

- 115g unsalted butter, softened
- 100g light brown sugar
- 50g caster sugar and 1 large egg
- 1 teaspoon vanilla extract
- 150g plain flour and Pinch of salt
- 1/2 teaspoon baking soda
- 100g chocolate chips

Instructions:

1. Preheat your Instant Vortex Plus Dual Air Fryer to 160°C (320°F).

2. In a mixing bowl, cream together the softened butter, brown sugar, and caster sugar until light and fluffy.

3. Add the egg and vanilla extract, and beat until well combined.

4. Sift in the flour, baking soda, and salt, then mix until a smooth dough forms.

5. Fold in the chocolate chips until evenly distributed throughout the dough.

6. Scoop tablespoon-sized portions of dough and roll them into balls.

7. Place the dough balls on a lined air fryer tray, leaving space between each one.

8. Flatten the dough balls slightly with the palm of your hand.

9. Air fry at 160°C (320°F) for 8-10 minutes, until the cookies are golden brown around the edges.

10. Once done, remove from the air fryer and let cool on a wire rack.

Nutritional Info (per cookie): Calories: 130 | Fat: 6g | Carbs: 18g | Protein: 1g

RASPBERRY CHEESECAKE CHIMICHANGAS

Prep: 15 mins | Cook: 10 mins | Makes: 6 chimichangas

Ingredients:

- 125g cream cheese, softened
- 1 teaspoon vanilla extract and 50g caster sugar
- 6 large flour tortillas and 50g granulated sugar
- 150g fresh raspberries
- 50g unsalted butter, melted
- 1 teaspoon ground cinnamon

Instructions:

1. Preheat your Instant Vortex Plus Dual Air Fryer to 180°C (350°F).
2. In a bowl, beat together the softened cream cheese, caster sugar, and vanilla extract until smooth.
3. Spread a generous spoonful of the cream cheese mixture onto each flour tortilla.
4. Place a few raspberries on top of the cream cheese mixture on each tortilla.
5. Fold the sides of each tortilla over the filling, then roll up tightly into a chimichanga shape.
6. In a shallow dish, mix together the granulated sugar and ground cinnamon.
7. Brush each chimichanga with melted butter, then roll in the cinnamon sugar mixture until coated.
8. Place the chimichangas in the air fryer basket, seam side down, leaving space between each one.
9. Air fry at 180°C (350°F) for 8-10 minutes, until golden brown and crispy.
10. Once done, remove from the air fryer and let cool slightly.

Nutritional Info (per chimichanga): Calories: 290 | Fat: 15g | Carbs: 34g | Protein: 4g

Prep: 20 mins | Cook: 10 mins | Makes: 24 churro bites

Ingredients:

- 125ml water and 1 large egg and

- 50g unsalted butter and 125g plain flour

- 1 tablespoon granulated sugar and 1/4 teaspoon salt

- 1/2 teaspoon vanilla extract and 50ml double cream

- 50g granulated sugar (for coating) and 100g dark chocolate, chopped

Instructions:

1. Preheat your Instant Vortex Plus Dual Air Fryer to 180°C (350°F).

2. In a saucepan, combine water, butter, sugar, and salt. Bring to a boil over medium heat.

3. Reduce heat to low and add flour all at once. Stir vigorously until the mixture forms a ball.

4. Remove from heat and let cool for 5 minutes.

5. Beat in the egg and vanilla extract until smooth and well combined.

6. Transfer the dough to a piping bag fitted with a large star tip.

7. Pipe small lengths of dough directly into the air fryer basket, cutting with scissors.

8. Air fry at 180°C (350°F) for 8-10 minutes, until golden brown and crispy.

9. In a shallow dish, mix together granulated sugar and ground cinnamon.

10. Toss the churro bites in the cinnamon sugar mixture until coated.

11. In a small saucepan, heat double cream until just simmering.

12. Add chopped dark chocolate to the cream and let it sit for 1 minute.

13. Stir until chocolate is melted and the sauce is smooth.

14. Serve churro bites warm with chocolate sauce for dipping.

Nutritional Info (per churro bite with sauce): Calories: 120 | Fat: 7g | Carbs: 13g | Protein: 2g

Prep: 15 mins | Cook: 25 mins | Makes: 12 bars

Ingredients:

- 150g plain flour

- 100g light brown sugar and 100g rolled oats

- 1/2 teaspoon baking powder

- 115g unsalted butter, melted

- 250g fresh blueberries

- 50g granulated sugar and Pinch of salt

- 1 tablespoon lemon juice

- 1 tablespoon cornstarch

Instructions:

1.   Preheat your Instant Vortex Plus Dual Air Fryer to 180°C (350°F).

2.   In a bowl, combine the plain flour, rolled oats, light brown sugar, baking powder, and salt.

3.   Add the melted butter to the dry ingredients and mix until crumbly.

4.   Press two-thirds of the mixture into the bottom of a greased square baking pan.

5.   In another bowl, toss together the blueberries, granulated sugar, lemon juice, and cornstarch until well coated.

6.   Spread the blueberry mixture evenly over the crumb base.

7.   Sprinkle the remaining crumb mixture over the top of the blueberries.

8.   Place the baking pan in the air fryer basket and air fry at 180°C (350°F) for 25-30 minutes, until the topping is golden brown and the blueberries are bubbling.

9.   Once done, remove from the air fryer and let cool completely before slicing into bars.

Nutritional Info (per bar): Calories: 180 | Fat: 8g | Carbs: 25g | Protein: 2g

Prep: 15 mins | Cook: 8 mins | Makes: 8 spring rolls

Ingredients:

- 4 large ripe bananas

- 8 spring roll wrappers

- 8 teaspoons Nutella

- Icing sugar, for dusting (optional)

Instructions:

1. Preheat your Instant Vortex Plus Dual Air Fryer to 180°C (350°F).

2. Peel the bananas and cut them in half crosswise, then slice each half in half lengthwise.

3. Place a teaspoon of Nutella on one end of each spring roll wrapper.

4. Place a banana slice on top of the Nutella, then roll up the wrapper, tucking in the sides as you go.

5. Seal the edges with a little water to prevent them from opening during cooking.

6. Place the banana spring rolls in the air fryer basket, seam side down, leaving space between each one.

7. Air fry at 180°C (350°F) for 8-10 minutes, until golden brown and crispy.

8. Once done, remove from the air fryer and let cool slightly before serving.

9. Dust with icing sugar, if desired, before serving.

Nutritional Info (per spring roll): Calories: 160 | Fat: 4g | Carbs: 30g | Protein: 2g

Prep: 10 mins | Cook: 10 mins | Makes: 8 crescent rolls

Ingredients:

- 1 tube (235g) refrigerated crescent roll dough

- 8 marshmallows

- 8 chocolate squares

- 2 tablespoons unsalted butter, melted

- 2 tablespoons granulated sugar

- 1 teaspoon ground cinnamon

Instructions:

1. Preheat your Instant Vortex Plus Dual Air Fryer to 180°C (350°F).

2. Unroll the crescent roll dough and separate into triangles.

3. Place a marshmallow and a chocolate square at the wide end of each dough triangle.

4. Roll up the dough tightly, enclosing the marshmallow and chocolate.

5. Brush the tops of the crescent rolls with melted butter.

6. In a small bowl, mix together the granulated sugar and ground cinnamon.

7. Sprinkle the cinnamon sugar mixture over the tops of the crescent rolls.

8. Place the crescent rolls in the air fryer basket, leaving space between each one.

9. Air fry at 180°C (350°F) for 8-10 minutes, until golden brown and puffed.

10. Once done, remove from the air fryer and let cool slightly before serving.

Nutritional Info (per crescent roll): Calories: 190 | Fat: 10g | Carbs: 22g | Protein: 2g

Prep: 15 mins | Cook: 30 mins | Serves: 8

Ingredients:

- 200g unsalted butter, softened

- 200g caster sugar

- 4 large eggs

- 1 teaspoon vanilla extract

- 200g self-raising flour

- Zest of 1 lemon

- Juice of 1/2 lemon

- 100g icing sugar

Instructions:

1.   Preheat your Instant Vortex Plus Dual Air Fryer to 160°C (320°F).

2.   In a mixing bowl, cream together the softened butter and caster sugar until pale and fluffy.

3.   Beat in the eggs, one at a time, followed by the vanilla extract.

4.   Sift in the self-raising flour and fold into the mixture until just combined.

5.   Stir in the lemon zest and juice until evenly distributed throughout the batter.

6.   Pour the batter into a greased loaf tin, spreading it out evenly.

7.   Place the loaf tin in the air fryer basket and air fry at 160°C (320°F) for 25-30 minutes, until golden brown and a skewer inserted into the center comes out clean.

8.   Once done, remove from the air fryer and let cool in the tin for 10 minutes before transferring to a wire rack to cool completely.

Nutritional Info (per slice): Calories: 310 | Fat: 16g | Carbs: 37g | Protein: 4g

PEANUT BUTTER CUP BLONDIES

Prep: 15 mins | Cook: 25 mins | Serves: 9

Ingredients:

- 100g unsalted butter, melted
- 150g light brown sugar
- 1 large egg
- 1 teaspoon vanilla extract
- 125g plain flour
- 1/2 teaspoon baking powder
- Pinch of salt
- 100g peanut butter cups, chopped

Instructions:

1. Preheat your Instant Vortex Plus Dual Air Fryer to 160°C (320°F).

2. In a mixing bowl, whisk together the melted butter and light brown sugar until smooth.

3. Beat in the egg and vanilla extract until well combined.

4. Sift in the plain flour, baking powder, and salt, then fold until just combined.

5. Fold in the chopped peanut butter cups until evenly distributed throughout the batter.

6. Pour the batter into a greased square baking pan, spreading it out evenly.

7. Place the baking pan in the air fryer basket and air fry at 160°C (320°F) for 20-25 minutes, until golden brown and set.

8. Once done, remove from the air fryer and let cool in the pan before slicing into squares.

Nutritional Info (per blondie): Calories: 250 | Fat: 12g | Carbs: 32g | Protein: 4g

Prep: 15 mins | Cook: 5 mins | Serves: 4

Ingredients:

- 250g strawberries, hulled

- 4 slices pound cake, cut into cubes

- 100g white chocolate, melted

- Wooden skewers

Instructions:

1. Preheat your Instant Vortex Plus Dual Air Fryer to 180°C (350°F).

2. Thread a strawberry onto a wooden skewer, followed by a cube of pound cake.

3. Repeat the process with remaining strawberries and cake cubes, alternating between them on the skewers.

4. Place the skewers in the air fryer basket, leaving space between each one.

5. Air fry at 180°C (350°F) for 4-5 minutes, until the pound cake is lightly toasted.

6. Once done, remove from the air fryer and drizzle with melted white chocolate before serving.

Nutritional Info (per serving): Calories: 220 | Fat: 10g | Carbs: 30g | Protein: 3g

RECIPE INDEX

Garlic Parmesan Breadsticks

Garlic Parmesan Chicken Wings

Herb-Roasted Whole Chicken

Homemade Chicken Nuggets with Honey Mustard Dip

Homemade Potato Chips with Dipping Sauce

Honey Garlic Glazed Salmon Fillets

Honey Glazed Ham Steaks

Honey Mustard Chicken Thighs

I

Italian Herb Chicken Parmesan

Italian Sausage and Peppers

J

Jamaican Jerk Chicken Thighs

Juicy Air Fryer Burgers with Cheese

L

Lemon Glazed Pound Cake Slices

Lemon Herb Salmon Fillets

Lemon Pepper Shrimp Skewers

Lemon Garlic Roast Chicken Drumsticks

M

Maple Glazed Bacon-Wrapped Pork Tenderloin

Mediterranean Roasted Eggplant Slices

Mediterranean Stuffed Trout with Feta and Olives

Mini Quiche Cups with Spinach and Cheese

Miniature Meatballs with BBQ Glaze

Molten Chocolate Lava Cakes

Moroccan Spiced Lamb Koftas

N

Nutella-Stuffed Banana Spring Rolls

CONCLUSION

As you reach the end of this comprehensive guide to air frying with the Instant Vortex Plus Dual Air Fryer, you'll undoubtedly feel empowered and inspired to embark on a culinary journey like no other. This versatile appliance has opened up a world of possibilities, allowing you to indulge in your favorite crispy treats while embracing a healthier lifestyle.

Throughout the pages of this cookbook, you've discovered an array of mouth-watering recipes that showcase the true potential of air frying. From classic comfort foods like crispy chicken wings and loaded potato skins to gourmet delights like coconut-crusted shrimp and herb-roasted whole chicken, each recipe has been carefully crafted to deliver maximum flavor and crispiness.

But this cookbook is more than just a collection of recipes; it's a comprehensive resource that equips you with the knowledge and skills to become an air frying master. The tips and tricks section has provided invaluable insights into the art of air frying, guiding you through techniques like preheating, arranging food for even cooking, and using seasonings to elevate flavors.

Air frying is more than just a cooking method; it's a lifestyle choice that promotes healthier eating habits without sacrificing flavor or satisfaction. With the Instant Vortex Plus Dual Air Fryer, you can indulge in your favorite crispy treats while feeling good about the choices you're making for yourself and your family.

As you close this cookbook, remember that the journey of air frying is far from over. Embrace the versatility of your Instant Vortex Plus Dual Air Fryer and let your culinary creativity soar. Experiment with new recipes, explore unique flavor combinations, and continue to discover the endless possibilities that this innovative appliance has to offer.

Printed in Great Britain
by Amazon

60337619R00067